A Safe Place to Begin

Rex Bradley is one of the directors of Spectrum, a centre for humanistic psychotherapy in London, which is also home to the Spectrum Incest Intervention Project, a charity that works with both adults and children who have been sexually abused, and aims to educate and raise awareness of childhood sexual abuse generally. The Spectrum Incest Intervention Project was founded by Terry Cooper and Jenner Roth, both of whom are also founder directors of Spectrum. Rex works with individuals, couples and groups at Spectrum in London and in his home town of Portsmouth.

Caroline Johnson-Marshall works as a teacher of children with special needs in inner London. She has worked with children with special needs for 17 years, initially for six years in a deprived area of Liverpool. Many of the children she worked with had been abused in many ways, including sexually. She has also run groups for people with eating disorders, and leads treks to Ladakh.

We would like to thank the people who
have contributed to this book by sharing
their experiences with us, and
especially Marion Russell for her faith
and enthusiasm in the project.

Rex Bradley & Caroline Johnson-Marshall

A Safe Place to Begin

*Working to Recover
from Childhood Sexual Abuse*

Rex Bradley and
Caroline Johnson-Marshall

Thorsons
An Imprint of HarperCollins*Publishers*

Thorsons
An Imprint of HarperCollins*Publishers*
77–85 Fulham Palace Road,
Hammersmith, London W6 8JB
1160 Battery Street,
San Francisco, California 94111-1213

Published by Thorsons 1993
10 9 8 7 6 5 4 3 2 1

A catalogue record for this book
is available from the British Library

ISBN 0 7225 2723 3

Typeset by Harper Phototypesetters Limited,
Northampton, England
Printed in Great Britain by
HarperCollinsManufacturing Glasgow

Contents

This book is dedicated to Terry Cooper and
Jenner Roth, founder directors of Spectrum,
and the men, women and children whose work
at Spectrum and the Spectrum Incest Intervention
project who made this book possible.

Introduction

In our work with both adults and children over the years we have become more and more aware of how many children and adults from every walk of life are affected by abuse. We have become increasingly aware of how prevalent sexual abuse is. Many people are now beginning to recognize the kinds of effects that are caused by abuse and also the effect that abuse has had on their own lives.

We are living in an abusive society. All the time abusive acts are perpetrated and too often accepted as normal or allowed to pass unremarked upon. For many who have been sexually abused, it is hard to separate out the strands of our history and be clear that we have been abused. It can be almost a surprise when it is pointed out to us that what we experienced was abuse.

For most of us it is also a deep relief to recognize sexual abuse and to understand finally what we have been struggling with over the years. Many of the people Caroline interviewed when writing this book had experienced this sense of relief when they had confirmation that what they had experienced was sexual abuse. For many it was the beginning of feeling able to look at and explore the pain and suffering that had been locked within them. In some cases we talked to people who were themselves already working with people who had been abused, but who had not yet acknowledged their own abuse and suffering.

This book is for all those who are suffering as a result of

abuse, sexual or otherwise. It is for those who may not even recognize that they have been abused and that their lives have been spoiled or saddened. Our aim is to help people to recognize where they have been abused in their own lives and to realize that they can do something about it.

We would like to see a greater awareness of the sexual abuse that continues to happen. We would also like to encourage people to recognize and fully acknowledge abuse in their own lives and in other people's and to speak out about it. It is only when a whole generation is clear and firm and able to make a stand that there is a chance of change.

We therefore encourage people to speak out about their own abuse whenever they can if it feels safe and appropriate to do so. By doing so they become part of the movement to break the collusive silence that we have lived with for centuries. We also want to challenge the disbelief that we have heard so many people express. So often relatives, family and neighbours tell themselves, 'This cannot be happening', and that he or she 'would never do a thing like that'. The reality is that it can happen; it is possible for it to be happening in every area, in every street in the land. There is still a denial of that reality, and abuse continues. Sometimes it continues in private and secrecy, and sometimes with active connivance.

We hear of cases where someone has been wrongly accused of sexually abusing children, and where people who have been attempting to help a child who has been sexually abused are affecting the child negatively. Our hope in writing this book is that abuse and the symptoms that go with it will be more quickly and more clearly recognized, and that people will respond to abused children more effectively.

Children are not born inherently bad, difficult or

troublesome. As small children we bring huge amounts of goodwill to our relationships with those around us. Even when the people in our lives continually hurt us, we want to be with them and to please them. Children learn very quickly and adjust themselves to hurtful behaviour as if that is all they can expect in relationships. Usually they hold very deeply the conviction that they are to blame for the hurt they are receiving. When we are small we try all the while to do our best – that is in our nature. We accept that what has happened to us is normal, that it's right and it's what we deserve. As we grow up we may begin to recognize it's wrong, but initially we try to find the fault in ourselves, and we come to believe it. We're not even conscious of making any internal adjustment. Feeling bad, we just get on and do the best we can.

As children we want and need our caretakers to love us. We want to be good girls or boys for them, and we will do almost anything to make them happy, no matter how painful it is for us or how unhappy it may make us in the short or long term. For many abused children, the attention they received when they were abused was the only way they were loved, the only form of contact that they had.

The experience of sexual abuse in early life has devastating effects on a child's emotional growth. Many people grow up feeling unable to say no or to assert themselves when they are in an abusive situation. Many people are unable even to recognize that they are being abused, they have such a low level of self-esteem. Many make poor relationships that are hurtful. They then may decide to stay in these abusive relationships. They may feel that, on balance, even a bad relationship is better than no relationship at all, or perhaps that this is as good a relationship as they can expect. This is an important decision, and we would like to encourage anyone in this situation to consider it with a more caring attitude towards themselves, and with information and support.

In this book we share with you some people's experiences of sexual abuse. We show that if you were sexually abused, and if you recognize what happened to you and take the time to deal with the pain and the memories that emerge, you can learn to live a happier, healthier life. Most importantly, you can raise your self-esteem so that you will not allow yourself to be abused again.

We would also like you to look at the abusive behaviour that you may have learned. It's easy to carry on abusing others, even in subtle ways, when you've been abused yourself. This is one of the ways that abuse is perpetuated.

If you have been sexually abused, you can learn how to take down the walls that you've built up over the years to cover up the pain and to defend yourself. You can feel positive and respectful about yourself again.

Most of all we have written this book because we want people to find what we have found, that by loving and caring for yourself you can recover from having been sexually abused. By learning to take the time to focus on your own needs properly, you can truly create a safe place for yourself. You can begin to see that you have a right to safety, and that you can say no to difficult and dangerous experiences if you want to. You can learn to use your own experiences and judgements to make 'a safe place to begin', and go on with your life from that safer place.

1. What is Abuse?

Imagine you have some information about yourself that you have always known and that you have accepted as just a part of your life. Then one day you are sitting in a therapy group and someone tells a very similar story to yours. You hear them say, 'This was abusive', or maybe the group leader says, 'That was abuse.' You suddenly realize that what happened to you was abuse and that someone you may have loved and trusted is an abuser. These are the kinds of insights that people everywhere are having now as the issue of childhood sexual abuse is shared more openly. The fact is that often we have grown up with a set of standards and values that have deceived or confused us, or we may simply have 'forgotten' about our history of abuse. We can have been sexually abused by a member of our family, by a stranger, or by a friend of the family, and just not have recognized it.

Suddenly a yawning gulf opens up between what you have always believed about yourself and your family and the reality as you now begin to understand it. You have been abused, perhaps many times over, and you didn't even know it.

Can we say that anyone has completely escaped some form of sexual abuse as they grow up?

If we look around us we can see sexually abusive behaviour and attitudes everywhere, and even publicly so. In shops and offices, pubs and restaurants, on public transport and at garages, molestation and abusive behaviour continues. People suffer indignities without feeling able to do anything about it or to change things. Sexual abuse and harassment, which occurs at so many different levels, is an enormous factor in our lives. Ranging from what might seem to be small incidents to the outrageous, it leaves so many people feeling helpless, powerless and bad.

Living in a society that allows any abusive behaviour to pass unremarked compounds the difficulty we experience in recognizing personal assault. So many people are deeply convinced that they must not make a fuss, that somehow it was their fault, or that it was normal for them to be treated like this. Abusive behaviour thrives on this kind of inhibition.

As children we are encouraged to believe in the rightness of our parents and so we feel unable to blame or question them. We therefore believe that whatever happens to us is somehow our own fault. We cannot bear to believe that our parents could be at fault.

It is especially difficult to acknowledge that those who form part of our own identity – our parents, caretakers or close relatives – have behaved shockingly and abusively and have seen us as sexual objects. As small children we need to believe that our parents are perfect. We feel we are dependent on them for survival, whether this is realistic or unrealistic. So when anything happens which feels bad, we take this feeling of badness into ourselves. We are not able to separate ourselves from our family situation and realize the truth of what is happening.

Many men and women have, as children, experienced deep fears around other people's sexual behaviours, and many people have experienced lasting damage because of sexual abuse. Unable to express their fear, distress, anger and confusion at the time that the abuse occurred, they hold this within themselves and it affects all their subsequent emotional development.

We would like you to be able to examine your own history and to make a decision for yourself about whether your life has been safe, or whether you too have suffered sexual abuse.

For instance, sexual abuse can be when the nice old man at the swimming baths who is helping you to learn to swim and is holding you up in the water begins to do something other than help you to swim. It's not just where his hand is, it's the fact that he is thinking of something other than you swimming, and you know it.

There is something strange now – he isn't helping, but harming. Things feel out of step – you're still innocent, but he isn't. The joy and excitement of working together on you learning how to swim – which you want to do so much – are gone, and a mixture of fear and unease and of not understanding begins taking their place. Worse, you may not sense anything at all at first, because you're wrapped up in what you are trying so hard to do. Eventually you do feel it, and, instead of thanking him with a smile and leaving, you have to try to ask him to let you go.

You may see him again, looking at you, maybe waving. You feel bad when you see him and when you think of him. Maybe you don't go swimming so much any more, or maybe not at all. You've learned a little not to trust, and some of your being a little child is gone.

Or perhaps you and your sister never get any love from your daddy. All he ever does is shout at you and sometimes he hits you really hard. You can remember a time when he hit your sister's head on the table really hard and upset all your younger brothers and sisters. He was very angry with her and said she was looking at the men at work.

Your mother was there, but she was powerless and didn't try to stop him. Most of the time your mummy stays in the sitting-room watching the television. She doesn't seem to know what's happening in her own kitchen, or in the bedroom that you and your sister share in the attic. If she does know, why doesn't she seem to mind? It all feels so wrong, it can't be right, can it?

Sometimes daddy comes home in a really good mood and you feel very frightened. A big lump sticks in your throat and your mummy tells you off for not eating your dinner. You can't eat it because you feel ill. Daddy calls you into the sitting-room. He's there all on his own and you know mummy won't come in and interrupt. He has his penis in his hand and he is rubbing it. He wants you to do it and he tells you that you are his special girls, you and your sister. You don't talk to the neighbours and you come straight home from school. He has brought your sister a nice new coat and you some sweets. You stroke his penis, even though you don't like to, because, for a little while, it does seem like he loves you. Apart from the odd times when you and your sister hold hands, and when the little ones play together with you, this is the only time you are loved by anyone. Most of the time you feel cold and sad and you feel you need to be loved a lot. Even your sister is distant most of the time, and you don't know why.

You get away from home and from the house as often as you can, and when you can you get a job away from home. You are still a child really, but you can't stay there, even though you feel scared and that you are abandoning the little ones. You go out into the world earlier than you should. You are a very shy person and you ache to be loved. You cannot stay at your home or even visit there for fear of the sitting-room and your father, the bully.

Sexual abuse also happens to boys. Maybe you don't see your dad much, because he works all the time. Sometimes you just get to see him when he comes in, and then your mum puts you to bed. Sometimes you don't see him because mummy puts you to bed before he comes home.

You spend a lot of time together, you and your mum, and sometimes she does something special with you. You know when it may happen because she puts on some lipstick and scent, and you know she means to be beautiful – but it still may not happen.

When she puts you to bed, if you really, really ask her nicely, not just once but many times, then she will lie with you on your single bed, in your bedroom, and tell you once that she loves you. And if you try really hard, she will kiss you once, on the mouth. You will taste her lipstick, smell her perfume and feel just the tip of her tongue in your mouth. This is a kiss no one else gives you, and you know you are more special to your mummy than daddy is. This means you can never have a proper relationship with your daddy ever again – you are the man in the house, you are seven years old, and you have a secret.

That secret shapes your sexuality for the rest of your life, as you look for that special feeling with partner after partner, all of whom want to be loved as themselves. You, however, want them to be like your mother. You may not even remember why. You just experience wanting something that you can't quite get.

As you can see, childhood sexual abuse is above all the theft of childhood, the cruellest theft of all, irredeemable, irreplaceable. Our childhood is a time when innocence and safety are needed, a time when we have a chance to establish who we really are, what we like, what we don't like, what our tastes and preferences are. When we are sexually abused, this child time is replaced by a childhood where happy times are overshadowed by memories of the abusive relationship, dread of the next time, or blankness, loss of memory and confusion.

As long ago as 1896, Sigmund Freud wrote a definition of sexual abuse in a paper entitled 'The Aetiology of Hysteria':

All the strange conditions under which the incongruous pair continue their love relations – on the one hand the adult, who cannot escape his share in the mutual dependence necessarily entailed by a sexual relationship, and who is at the same time armed with complete authority and the right to punish, and can exchange the one role for the other to the uninhibited satisfaction of his whims, and on the other hand the child, who in his helplessness is at the mercy of this arbitrary use of power, who is prematurely aroused to every sort of sensibility and exposed to every sort of disappointment, and whose exercise of the sexual performances assigned to him is often interrupted by his imperfect control of his natural needs – all these grotesque and yet tragic disparities distinctly mark the later development of the individual and of his neurosis, with countless permanent effects which deserve to be traced in the greatest detail.

Freud later retracted his statements about childhood sexual abuse. People were not yet willing to accept its prevalence, and were in too great a state of denial even to contemplate the truth in Freud's definition. Freud himself also came to deny it. He eventually said that the early memories that his patients uncovered and revealed to him were in fact fantasies, stemming from their desires rather than their actual experiences.

This was a maddening double denial: first, that they had not really experienced what they shared with Freud; and then that, rather than being the victims of the situation, they had unconsciously desired the experiences and made them up. Freud's modified ideas about the sexual abuse of children, and his denial of the effects of that abuse, have shaped psychiatry and psychoanalysis for the larger part of this century. They have also contributed significantly to the suppression of the truth about sexual abuse.

The generally accepted attitude towards children has been that they should not be believed and that they are untrustworthy. Until recently children have been taught that they must respect and obey adults and do what they are told, regardless of how the adults behave towards them. For the first time in history, we are beginning to talk openly about incest and childhood sexual abuse. Society has not been ready until now to look at this issue and take it on. Although things are changing, the fact is that a lot of people still don't realize or feel able to acknowledge that they have been abused.

We believe that it's important to begin to enlarge the picture of what may constitute abuse. For instance, reaching a certain age does not necessarily mean we can give informed consent, or that with consent a sexual relationship is not abusive. An awful lot of adults, as well as children, are not emotionally free to give their consent to sexual activity. Having learnt about sex through abusive relationships, they reach for the familiar in relationships that are likely to harm them further and compound the damage already done.

Manipulation, guilt, pressure from peers or parents, lack of personal power or knowledge – all these can make it impossible to make healthy decisions when giving consent. Any sexual act entered into where one of the parties is unable to give their consent from a position of self-worth is potentially abusive.

Children who are locked into abusive family situations have to deny their own experience. Little children become confused; they need love and tenderness, but feel disturbed and frightened by what is happening. This may not be just in their relationship with the abuser, but with all the people who let the abuse happen and who seem to be condoning it by their avoidance and silence, making it seem like the child's own fault. An older child may know that what is going on is wrong, but knows no expectation of freedom, rescue or reparation.

Abuse confuses so many things. Our natural needs for warmth, love and comfort are reluctantly but firmly abandoned in the face of an abusive relationship. It is as if the personality exists still, but it exists behind a veil – a veil which affects the view of the world from inside at least as disastrously as the view of the person from outside. People who have been abused often have a real difficulty in making themselves understood and become very vulnerable to further abuse of all kinds.

So before you condemn someone as stupid or incompetent, stubborn or uncommunicative, ask yourself: were they abused as a child? Many people were, and the damage can last for a lifetime. And before you condemn yourself for being slow, clumsy, or difficult in relationships, consider your own history. If you were sexually abused as a child then you will have been affected by it in many different ways.

We feel enraged at seeing clients who are still confused, clearly lacking self-esteem, not knowing where they stand, where they want to be, or what they want to do – people who are fearful of being in a relationship and somehow cannot allow this in their lives, however hard they may seem to try, although they desperately want love, warmth and comfort.

Older people, years after being abused, are still struggling to find their rightful place in their life, their skills muted, ambition withheld, the pattern of abuse repeated over and over again.

Many people have been wounded and hurt as children and carry with them the memories and secrets, the feelings of guilt and a terrible sense of shame that colours and distorts their relationships for life.

We hope that more people will come to recognize sooner their experiences of abuse and to acknowledge them fully, however much they may have minimized them in the past. We all need to come to realize the sufferings and pains we went through as children and learn to know our feelings rather than numbness and defensiveness. There is no justification for abusive behaviour, and it is time for the denial to end. The effects on an abused child affect us all, one abused child is an abusive society.

2. Effects of Childhood Sexual Abuse

All childhood abuse, whether it is physical, emotional or sexual, causes damage to the child. There are, however, specific effects that stem from being sexually abused. These effects are complicated, and sometimes surprising.

The effects of having been sexually abused as a child begin to show in childhood, either when the abuse first begins or shortly afterwards. It goes on to affect our feelings about ourselves in all situations – how we live, and who we are in the world.

Human responses do, of course, vary tremendously. We are all complex, sensitive and creative – that is a natural part of being an 'ordinary' human being. We all react in our own unique, individual ways to things that happen to us, including sexual abuse.

If you have been abused and we were to ask you about the effects of that, you may, or may not, be able to say what they are. You may be able to describe the feelings – anger, confusion, sadness or grief. Some people know clearly what effects the abuse has had on them, others have no idea. This chapter chronicles many of the effects of sexual abuse. Some of these effects you may recognize in yourself; others may not apply to you at all.

One thing is certain: when we are affected in childhood by sexual abuse, and if that abuse is not dealt with, it will surface over and over again in our lives until it is addressed. Rex worked with a six-year-old girl, whom we will call Amy, who was confused and angry, as well as sad, from having been sexually abused by her father. Her parents had split up six months before, after an increasingly difficult and angry period where the mother had been emotionally and physically abused. The father had just begun having access to the children again, and this obviously affected all the relationships in the family. The children were frightened that things would go back to the angry and violent scenes that they had witnessed before, while at the same time they wanted to see their daddy again.

In the confusion it was a while before the mother realized that something very odd had begun to happen.

Once he returned to the family, the father manipulated Amy into performing oral sex for him. She didn't like it, although she pretended to her father that she did. She was frightened, and did what her daddy wanted in order to keep him happy. She didn't want him to be angry and violent with her, and she wanted the family to be as safe and as ordinary as she could make it. Her four-year-old sister Susan saw the sexual abuse happen several times and was deeply affected by what she saw.

An effect that his manipulations had on Amy was that she began to display behaviour that could be described as 'sexual'. The sexual pressure on Amy changed her whole view of her world, and the people in it, at the age of six.

Family friends came to visit the home and noticed that she had become much more affectionate with men. These friends didn't feel comfortable with her behaviour, because there was a sexual edge to it. She would look at men's genital area, sometimes touch them there, and she played seductive games with them. None of this had been part of her behaviour before this time. She also began to show much less interest in the women who came to the house.

She was cold with them where before she had obviously wanted their affection and reassurance.

Amy's sister Susan also changed. She became angry and less affectionate to Amy. They began to argue and fight a lot more than they had before. Their mother often heard them arguing about who was most loved by their daddy. She talked to them and it quickly became clear that their father was being sexual with Amy.

The sexual abuse separated two children who had previously been quite close. Amy felt bad about what was going on, but also felt she had to defend herself against her sister's angry allegations that daddy didn't really love her because he was doing something dirty with her. To retaliate, Amy had told Susan that daddy only did it with her because he liked her best. This left her very confused, as she was having to pretend that she was happy doing something which she disliked and which frightened her.

Susan was feeling left out. She was dealing with her feelings by saying that daddy didn't really love Amy as he was doing dirty things with her. The feeling of being 'left out' of sexual abuse is very common in a family where abuse is taking place. Older survivors of family sexual abuse that we have talked to can remember this terrible dilemma – wanting to belong, and yet not wanting to be abused.

When the mother and the two daughters first came to see Rex, the session seemed to go very well. There were simple introductions, then some time was spent deciding who would sit where in the room in an attempt to have both the children feel at ease. We then discussed what had happened with daddy. Mummy said that she wasn't happy about it, and the children said that they were unhappy about it too.

The children got on well with each other in the session.

23

They talked about being angry with one another, and also about being frightened by what daddy was doing with them. We decided that what their daddy was doing wasn't nice for either of them, and that it wasn't their fault. By the end of the session they seemed to be less competitive with each other. They had felt good talking together and with Rex about what had happened with daddy.

We decided to meet again in a week's time, and also that their daddy shouldn't visit, at least until after then, as no one felt safe with him at the moment.

Afterwards, everyone said goodbye, but then Amy came running back up the stairs on her own, put her head against Rex's genital area, and made kissing and licking noises. She said goodbye in a cheery voice and ran off back down the stairs again to her mother and sister. Rex and the girls' mother were both shocked. It was a very real confirmation of all that the girls had talked about in the session, and a clear example of how this 'training' in sexual behaviour had deeply affected Amy.

She was now very vulnerable in a number of ways. Some adults encountering Amy's behaviour might have punished her or made her feel bad. If she had been punished, perhaps by her mother, imagine the confusion and outrage she could have felt. For Amy it would mean that she was being taught one day by one parent that a certain behaviour is good, and then being punished for it the next day by her other parent. It would be only too easy for Amy to have been labelled, perhaps as 'promiscuous' and 'over-sexed', when the reality is that her behaviour was coming from her experience of having been sexually abused.

So far we have looked at what effect the abuse was having on Amy in the context of her family. But think for a minute about what could have happened if Amy had behaved as she did with Rex with another man, for example with someone who would see that behaviour as a 'come on' from a six-year-old girl. Then imagine the confusion and the sense of being out of control if that person began to respond sexually to her. Just think what could happen to her if she did that with someone who would take advantage of a child.

The fact is that situations like that do happen to children who have been abused, over and over again, with many terrible outcomes. One important thing to recognize about the devastating effects of sexual abuse is that it makes children much more vulnerable to further abuse, sexually and in every other way. Children who have been sexually abused are more confused about what is right and what is wrong, and in their confusion they are even less able to protect themselves.

Luckily for Amy, her mother believed her and asked for help to deal with the situation, which meant that the whole issue could be brought to light, talked about in a safe place with a person who was clear, caring and trustworthy, and dealt with. Amy, her mother and her sister worked in therapy and the father was completely excluded from seeing the children until both the mother and children felt safe enough to allow him supervised access. He was not allowed to spend any time alone with the children.

Two years later, Amy and Susan are well and happy and have resumed a similar relationship to the one they had together before they were sexually abused. The mother's self-esteem is higher, and she has gone back to college part time to obtain qualifications. Mum, Amy and Susan feel good about what they worked through in their therapy together. They seem generally to get on with one another, and having worked together has given them more sense of their own power. This is in contrast to when the abuse was happening, when they were in conflict with one another. Then they were confused, fragmented, frightened, angry and powerless.

The father still comes to see the children from time to time. He is never left alone with Amy and Susan. He has never worked on his own behaviour, which makes the rest of the family angry with him, and helps to keep him different and separate from them. He seems content to carry on with a self-destructive life-style.

If Amy and Susan continue to grow up in a family where these issues can be talked about and shared, they will be able to carry on with their own emotional development. If and when the memories arise again, they will be able to discuss them, and there is no reason why they should ever have to be in therapy again. They will be able to process their feelings and thoughts with the help of the people around them.

We know that this is not usually the case – most children will need outside help in dealing with sexual abuse. As they grow up children need help and support to look again and again at what happened to them, with and without professional help; and when they have grown up, as adults, the need is the same.

A woman who would like to be known as Istra was abused as a small child. Istra had two older brothers, one of whom, in rough games, would put his finger into her vagina, and both of whom would bully her continually, as she was the smallest and most vulnerable child in the family. They learnt this behaviour from their parents, who were both physically violent to their children. Their father, who dominated the household in a brutal way, would lash out at any of them at any time and also at his wife. Their mother had very severe emotional problems that led to spells in a psychiatric hospital. She would frequently hit her children with a poker and behave in a very disturbed way. Istra grew up feeling that no one would ever support her or take her side or protect her from the violence she experienced.

The family used to spend their holidays with the maternal grandmother and Istra was often sent off to spend time with their neighbour, whom we shall call Mr S., down by his allotment. Mr S. would talk to Istra about his vegetables and how they grew, and gradually he began to talk more about things such as the difference between cows and bulls, and about Istra's growing body, which made Istra feel very uncomfortable. She sensed that there was something very wrong about it. These conversations went on for several summers as, despite Istra's continual protests and unhappy feelings about it, her parents would tell her to go and see Mr S. at each visit.

One summer Mr S. told Istra to tickle his 'little white mouse', and he fondled Istra's vagina and other parts of her body. He also kissed her on the mouth, forcing his tongue into her mouth.

Istra remembers having very little expectation of any support from her mother, but she went to her mother and told her. Her mother's reaction was to slap her face and scream at her never to say those things or Mr S. would lose his job and his wife would starve.

Istra remembers feeling distraught that her mother did not believe her. However, she did a very resourceful thing. She told the younger of her brothers. She knew it was very important that somebody should witness the abuse so that they could actually acknowledge that it happened, and that she was telling the truth.

She bribed her brother, who was two years older than she was, with some money and sweets. He went and hid in the cabbage patch and watched Mr S. abuse Istra. For many years only Istra and her brother knew about the abuse, but Istra feels that her brother's confirmation of what was happening to her stopped her from going out of her mind. It also enabled her to feel in some way in control in an environment that was out of control. She was doing the only thing that she could think of, as an eight-year-old girl, to make any sense out of her acutely distressing experiences.

As a child her feelings were never listened to or respected. A small child cannot see her feelings as separate from herself – her feelings *are* herself. So Istra felt that her very self was not worth listening to or deserving of respect. The message she got from her parents was that she did not have any rights and that her feelings were not important. As a small child she carried a terrible burden of feeling inadequate and worthless and that she could be used by others while her own needs were disregarded.

At the age of 13 Istra changed her name to help put all the feelings, behaviours and vulnerability that went with being a small child behind her. She disowned the part of herself that was a vulnerable little girl.

Because she was not able to make relationships in which she revealed anything about her hidden inner world, and because she was not able to trust people, she developed ways of surviving and relating that avoided intimacy. One result of this way of coping was that, until her late twenties when she started to have therapy, Istra continually got herself into abusive relationships which repeated the relationships that she had when she was a child. She felt dependent on her abusive partners. Although she seemed tough and strong she was actually unable to leave them or ask them to leave, even though they were clearly abusive to her.

She feels that being brought up in an environment where women were treated as second-class citizens contributed to her chronically low sense of self-esteem. For many years she wished she had been born a man. In her experience men were powerful, went out into the world and earned money, and also ruled the household, whereas women stayed in the home and worked and were victims.

As many abused children do, Istra may also have been identifying with her aggressors so that she herself would feel more powerful. In some way she might then be able to have some measure of control in her life and defend herself against the danger that men had come to represent to her. For Istra, vulnerability and softness came to represent weakness; these feelings were unacceptable and she despised them in herself, just as she herself had been despised. She did not feel safe if she allowed herself to feel vulnerable. The only way that she could feel strong was if she acted as if she was the more powerful person in the relationship, even though she was actually dependent.

Leila, who like Istra was brought up in a household where men were dominant, also suffered from a feeling of being powerless as a woman. An elderly uncle whom her family visited on family holidays used to greet her with a very sexual kiss and would fondle her breasts. At the time she found herself hardly able to believe that it was happening and denied her own experience. She thought she must be imagining it, even though it went on for several years.

Leila's father had a job that took him away for long periods. He was very rarely at home until, eventually, he left for good. Leila and her mother lived with two uncles who teased Leila mercilessly, most frequently about her body, which started to develop at a very early age. She remembers feeling completely powerless and that nobody would take her seriously or believe her. From a young age she felt that she was always going to be misinterpreted and 'played around with'. Nobody ever took her side and she had no expectation that anybody would.

Leila was also abused in her early teens by two of the owners of a riding stables she went to. Both of the men molested her when she was in the stables on her own with the horses. She never spoke about it or protested because she didn't think that anyone would believe her, and indeed she hardly believed it herself.

In the case of one of these abusive men there was a very uncomfortable kind of pay-off, or benefit, for Leila, in that she became his 'special girl' whom he took for rides in his car and whom he half promised to buy a horse. So if Leila had made any kind of a fuss she would have lost all kinds of privileges. And she wanted to feel special – she didn't want the abuse, but she so much wanted all the other things that went with it. In her life now, Leila still tends to minimize this abuse and the effect it had on her life; she still feels guilty and that in some way she was responsible.

As Leila's father was absent for so much of her life, this man at the stables had a very powerful and also very confusing influence on her. Her father had never been around to look after her or to protect her, and in later life she spent a lot of time seeking a father figure in her sexual relationships.

In her later teens Leila heard an aunt of hers talking to

her mother about having gone to stay with the abusive uncle and his wife when she was young. The aunt recalled falling and grazing her knee. The uncle, looking at the graze, pulled her skirt up to her waist. In her mid-thirties Leila talked to her mother about her uncle's abusive behaviour. Her mother replied that she knew about it because the uncle did it to her and to another aunt as well. When Leila asked why they didn't try to stop it, her mother said she was concerned that her uncle's wife would have been upset. Leila feels that it would have been most appropriate for her mother and her aunt to have contacted the uncle and to have said that if he didn't stop his abusive behaviour they would tell his wife.

Leila realized that her mother had felt just as powerless as she herself had done. Leila had therefore been brought up to believe that being a woman meant being a victim and that you were powerless to do anything. She had never had a sense of having rights. She had never felt that she had a right to pleasure in her own body, or control over who touched her body. She could not believe that she could have a satisfying sex life that was in any way directed by her. In every area of her life she felt that men held the power and that women were servile and powerless.

Through her work on herself in therapy, she realises how much her uncle's behaviour affected her and added to the difficulties she experienced in her emotional and physical development within a family where there was great confusion about sexuality. She remembers feeling a terrible sense of guilt about physically developing as she was growing up. The attitudes that Leila grew up with were expressed in such phrases as 'If you don't stop men they will go all the way', and 'It's a man's job to try and it's a woman's job to stop him.' When she was nine she heard her father say, 'Rape is impossible because a woman with her skirt up runs faster than a man with his trousers down.' Her mother's implicit and explicit messages were that for a woman to be sexual at all was not permissible. Leila feels that her guilt about the abuse she suffered is very much confused with a huge sense of guilt about being a sexually developing woman in such a background.

Leila, who is now in her forties, still struggles with being taken seriously, with taking herself seriously, and with believing her own experience. She says, 'I think I still don't really believe that I can have satisfying, self-directed sexual relationships, or that I have the right to ask for things, demand things and say no to the things I don't like. I'm not good at doing it clearly; I think I hedge around things. And I still don't feel good about my body.'

Leila has had to value herself enough to be able to make a positive commitment to herself. Most sexually abused people are severely lacking in any sense of their own worth. Rather, they see themselves as having value only as sexual objects, a lesson that they have learned in the most traumatic way.

Leila has a tendency to have relationships with younger men and she has always made sure that she is in no way dependent on them. She feels that this gives her a sense of power and control. It has also meant that she hasn't chosen partners who can nurture or protect her, and this is a repetition of a pattern that began in childhood. As a child, Leila wasn't nurtured or protected and she had no experience of men being able to give her what she so very much needed. She learned not to expect this at any level. Rather, she learned to expect abusive behaviour from men. In consequence, she has always experienced great difficulty in asking others to do things for her and in believing that she has any right to do so. She did not learn to value herself enough to feel that she was worthy of others' consideration and respect.

Roger was abused by a number of the people who lived in the boarding house where he grew up, first by his foster-father, who ran the place, and then by a woman lodger and her daughter. There was a chronic sense for him that anyone could come in and out of his life, that some of them abused him, and that when they did it was painful and difficult, but that it was to be expected. At no time did he feel that his foster-parents demanded very much respect for themselves in any way, and consequently he had no expectation that he would be respected either. The effect of this was that he was chronically abused throughout his childhood and through his early teens.

One incident he remembers that sums up how vulnerable he was to abuse happened at a derelict building where he was playing with his school friends. A man suddenly jumped out and made a grab for some of the children, including Roger. The others all ran off, but the man told Roger to stay, and he did.

Roger's foster-parents had always taken the side of teachers rather than Roger. Every time he had been in trouble with any authority they had said he must have brought it on himself by doing something wrong.

So Roger did as he was told, and stayed. The man made him pull down his short trousers and then sexually abused him. This went on for about 20 minutes, but it felt like a lifetime to Roger. As it ended, the man told him that he knew where Roger lived and that if he dared to tell anyone, he would kill him. Roger believed him, and never told anyone about the incident until he told his therapist

25 years later. This was not a conscious choice. Roger buried the experience immediately, and it stayed buried until after some years of therapy part of him finally felt safe enough to let it out.

When Roger came out of the house after the abuse, his friends had run away. He met them soon after, and they asked what had happened and why he hadn't run too. He lied and said the man had grabbed him; he was too ashamed to admit that he had been stupid and had stayed to be abused. He said that nothing had happened to him, and that the man had just let him go. The incident was soon forgotten, but Roger now had another guilty secret that he was keeping.

The woman lodger who abused him was seen as a prostitute by the people who lived in the street, and the house was regarded as a 'red light' house. Although the woman eventually moved out, Roger felt this atmosphere of disapproval and suspicion in the street about his house and his family and he believed that it was something to do with him. He felt bad about himself as he grew up, and his experiences of being abused over and over again seemed to confirm to him that he was bad.

It was only as Roger grew up and began to rebel against authority and not care about how the people in the street saw him that he began to have a level of self-esteem that enabled him to take a position for himself and stop the sexual abuse. He had a chronic problem with low self-esteem, and this was an issue that he needed to work on in therapy later in his life.

Our sexuality is reflected in all the parts of our lives. It is not a small part of us. It is part of our essential being. When our sexuality is abused in our early years, a huge part of our selfhood is affected in a way that will have negative effects on all our other stages of growth.

Being sexually abused is often the small child's first conscious sexual experience. Sex becomes a confusion of bad feelings about love and power, anger and humiliation, sadness and pain. It changes the whole world of a child, and as the child grows up and becomes an adult, they can live all their lives as if the world is not a safe place to be.

When we are sexually abused as a child, we are overwhelmed by the experience. We can't put it in perspective and we can't make judgements about it. It is a felt experience, a very large one, and it swamps us. We are unable to make sense of it. The body is experiencing something the mind won't or can't think about. We sometimes lock this away inside us in a way that means even we cannot find it or remember it. The trauma lives on in our body, and when we deny our feelings it is impossible for us to feel truly alive.

The experience of having been sexually abused continues to exist within us as both a chronic issue and an acute problem, surfacing in many different ways from time to time throughout our lives.

Loss of Childhood

There is a cliff edge that we cross when we are abused. We are torn from our childhood innocence and the sense that basically the world is a safe place, even though we have to be careful of some things and some people. When we are abused, no matter how trivial the experience, we no longer feel safe. There is a deep mistrust that is very difficult to get over. As an abused child, we go inside ourselves. Where there may have been openness, there is a sense of closing down and withdrawing.

Unsurprisingly, we feel a great unspoken need to protect ourselves. If the parents or grown-ups in our life cannot protect us from being hurt and abused in this way, or may even be the cause of our distress, then ultimately we have to take care of our own small selves. We have no other choice. So in order to take care of our own feelings, no matter how crudely or inadequately, we begin to parent ourselves and protect ourselves as best we can.

So often, the abused child is seen as wise beyond her or his years, an old head on young shoulders. We have to become 'adult' at a very young age. There is a loss of childhood in the sense that we cannot relax and enjoy our childhood and the protection of our parents.

This can show in our belief that even the people who are most important to us cannot really be trusted. We carry on treating people with suspicion when they try to get close to us, never knowing when an attempt to love us will become an attempt to abuse and control us.

We may begin to act inappropriately sexually, or become withdrawn, confused and silent. We may become 'less intelligent' than we were, or more 'bookish', finding some safety and security in being alone with ourselves.

Repetition of Abuse

Adults who were abused as children often have acutely low self-esteem. There is a deep feeling that there must be something wrong with them because of what happened to them.

People who grow up with such a small sense of their own

36

self-worth and with very little, if any, self-confidence have chronic difficulties when they go out into the world and have to meet people and make relationships. Having so little sense of self-worth means that their own sense of having rights and creating useful boundaries is very damaged. They are open to being continually abused because they don't recognize abuse and often think it is their fault anyway. They cannot easily identify the kind of person or behaviour that is harmful to them, only that something does not feel good.

So a clear outcome of sexual abuse is the likelihood of being abused again. Research shows that any sexually abused child is *four times* more likely to be sexually abused again than another child who has not been sexually abused.

We become less aware of and less able to resist all abuse, whether it is physical, emotional or sexual. Feelings about our own sexuality will be affected. We may feel a need to repeat punishment, pain and humiliation. We become more vulnerable to being exploited or bullied.

Blaming Ourselves

Because of our shock and confusion we often question ourselves rather than others. As children we cannot allow ourselves to believe that the people who are supposed to be loving and caring for us can be wrong, and so we learn to take the responsibility onto ourselves.

It's almost reassuring to think that what is happening is our fault. It can make us feel that we are in control instead of totally powerless, even though the reality is that we do not have power in this situation.

The feeling of guilt may also be more bearable to us than the awful feeling that our caretakers could do anything so terrible to us. We are likely to become introspective and passive, believing we are the ones who are in the wrong, rather than our persecutors. Inside us, we think *we* must be bad. We are often told that we are bad in other situations, so perhaps this is our fault too?

Because we are weakened, we can compensate, bluster or be aggressive, or be cowardly and subservient and unable to take a positive position for ourselves. Feeling guilty and bad becomes a way of life for us.

It's all too easy for children with already critically low self-esteem to change their bad feelings about what is happening outside them into believing that the badness is *inside* them, and that *they* are bad. They may have a deep fear that at any time they may be confronted with their being, or being seen as, bad. This sense of 'badness' is not necessarily carried consciously. The person may apparently feel perfectly all right about themselves, but in fact this feeling, however suppressed, of being a 'bad person' underlies everything they do.

This behaviour, begun in childhood, carries on through the person's life, and becomes less and less congruent with their current reality. They never were 'bad' in fact, but they carry on acting as if they are. This conviction is what we seek to undo as we work on ourselves. We need to replace those bad feelings with specific information about ourselves, and we need to replace that 'acting' bad with genuine actions which are true to who we are and what we really feel about a situation or relationship. This can take a long time. Deep-rooted beliefs and feelings don't change quickly.

Emotional Rigidity

As we grow, we carry the hurt and damaged child inside us. We deal with that child part in the best way we can. The emotional damage that the abuse has wrought has affected our growth and interfered with our development processes.

What seems to happen is that we become rigid. We get stuck in particular feelings or in a particular way of looking at the world. Maybe we joke a lot, or perhaps fear is our dominant emotion. Perhaps we want only to be soft and loving. Obviously, if this is how we are feeling, then it is fine to show that emotion. However, if all we are able to feel or express is a limited range of emotions, then something is wrong. We can end up with a preferred emotion, a preferred way of being in the world, and we are unable to be spontaneous.

We may not even notice our rigidity, but others do. We may be aware only of a vague sense of dissatisfaction, while others feel uncomfortable around us in a variety of ways.

We become rigid in our thinking and tend to see both people and situations as either positive or negative, good or bad, with no middle ground. We may often blame others unnecessarily, directing our bad feelings and suppressed anger at others instead of at the original cause.

Most of us know people who are almost always angry about something, or always sad, or always complaining about other people, seeming unable to find a good word to say about anyone. Sometimes it is really appropriate to be angry, and sometimes to be sad, but these people are stuck in a particular emotion. They have little or no choice about how to react in a given situation.

This behaviour is often a defence against feeling other

emotions which they would find threatening, especially as the feelings themselves could lead to re-experiencing an aspect of some earlier abuse. For example, someone who is angry, or critical and complaining, may have great difficulty in getting in touch with their sadness and hurt, apparently never needing anyone, and able to stand alone. This can make it very difficult for this person to have a lasting and balanced personal relationship, where there is always a need for us to be vulnerable from time to time.

Another person may be always sad, or continually having a lot of problems. Such people seem to be completely unable to stand on their own two feet. They may have great difficulty in contacting their anger and therefore be unlikely to take a position for themselves. As a result they will often be put upon, and suffer further abuse.

In this way, childhood sexual abuse brings out, magnifies, or distorts what is already there in our personality. A strong child may deal with the abuse by being strong, or by denying that it happened. They may also deny their needs, or deny the effects of the abuse. A child who tends to collapse and withdraw may do that more extremely than before. It is impossible to be exact or specific, as we are complex individuals. We will deal with our own experience of abuse in our own individual way.

Isolation

The sense of 'unfinished business' – feelings of anger, shame or sadness which the person does not consciously recognize, or which they feel they cannot deal with – can lead to their living a 'private life'. They feel very separate from others, depressed and angry by turns, and have no sense of there being a way out for them.

We may also simply over-react to a situation which touches on a felt memory. We might over-react where people seem to be like our abuser, or where the feeling is the same as when the abuse happened to us. We may then act as if we are in danger when in fact we are not, and push people away. This can have very difficult consequences. Where we have a chance to reflect on our reactions, and to see if we can separate out the fact from our fears, then we have an opportunity to behave differently.

Control

There can also be a need for a strong sense of control in adults who were abused as children, so that awkward, painful and 'difficult to handle' feelings can be kept at bay. There is a real need to deny their pain. Giving up control will mean facing the pain. The need for control can also show up in rigid demands that partners, children and others also keep *their* feelings hidden safely away, and control *their* emotions carefully.

Another manifestation of the need for control is compulsive behaviour, like obsessive cleaning and tidiness, excessive fussiness, and a need to get things right at any cost, whether at work or at home. An anxious need to be in control is also often present in relationships.

Dependence and Insecurity

Often, a strong sense of insecurity or unworthiness and a dependency on other people's love or goodwill for acceptance underlie the way adult survivors of sexual abuse make and attempt to maintain their relationships. Of course, anyone living in a relationship with this degree of dependence and insecurity is open to further abuse. All too often the request 'please be nice to me', whether it is spoken or unspoken, is seen by the partner as an invitation to take some advantage in the relationship. People who have been abused themselves tend to choose partners who have also been abused in some way, and who have further problems of their own. In these relationships, getting clear about what each person really feels and needs is vital if the relationship is to survive and be nourishing and supportive.

Ambivalence

Another effect of being sexually abused as a child occurs when the abuser is also a loving parent for most of the time. In wanting still to be loved, we may protect our abuser by not telling, or we may even pretend that we like what's happening. Or possibly we see the abuser as having a weakness that we must put up with from time to time, regarding the abuse as an aberration. We may feel that not making a fuss is better than 'being difficult', especially if we feel we may not be believed anyway. We can choose to feel guilty and blame ourselves rather than admit the truth about what happened to us.

We may then carry the terrific ambivalence that comes from this disturbing relationship on through our lives. We may never relax and feel safe with those we love, and perhaps never allow ourselves to be emotionally supported because of our constant fear that our loved one will once again become our abuser.

Ambivalence can by its nature really disable us. We will believe that anything that seems good can contain bad, and vice versa. The result in us can be a state of apathy, as we do not know which way to turn. We do not feel we have any effective choice.

Identifying with the Abuser

Instead of staying with the feeling of having been a victim, some of us feel much more identified with the aggressor, or perpetrator. We take comfort from recognizing ourselves as powerful rather than seeing ourselves as victims, although we would deny being perpetrators of any sort.

We may use anger as a dominant emotion, blaming others, telling ourselves it's all their fault. We spend our time being angry with the wrong people. In this way we defend ourselves against the underlying feeling of danger, and the fear that we may be abused again.

A child who is sexually abused can often be sexual with other children, for a variety of reasons. It can be an angry gesture – 'this happened to me, so I'm going to make it happen to you.' Or it can be a confused way of trying to share the experience, trying to make sense of the pain and humiliation of the abuse by bringing it into the child's world under her or his control. It can simply be that the child found the abuse pleasurable and wants to do it again, or that they want their child friend to feel what they felt, whether that was good or bad.

We must always be aware that it is never the child's fault. There is no moral shortcoming in children; they learn what they live. We need to be absolutely clear about this in order for us to look compassionately at what the effects were on us as children and as the adults we have become.

Abusing Our Bodies

We may also have contempt for our body, and self-loathing. We may abuse ourselves rather than giving our body the care and respect it deserves. We can abuse our body in many ways: by over or undereating, by alcohol or drug abuse, or by physically abusing ourselves. Or we may simply ignore our body's needs.

We need to work our way back to being the whole person we once were. When we integrate good feelings about our bodies, our rediscovered self-esteem and our feelings and emotions, then we will feel truly alive.

'Splitting' and Multiple Personalities

When we are abused as children we may split off from what is happening to us. We go to another place in ourselves under this terrific stress because we are not able to take on the fact that this terrible thing is happening. It is too much for us – beyond our nightmares, beyond anything we have ever known. We cannot comprehend it, so we go into shock and split off from the horror of what is happening.

Many people report a strong sense of leaving their bodies when they were being sexually abused. They sometimes report being able to 'look down on themselves' or see themselves in the situation as if from outside. We think this moving away and losing contact with the self is another example of splitting off, perhaps one of many shock responses that can become habitual and repeated.

It has become clear to many practitioners, and to many who have been sexually abused and severely traumatized as children, that this splitting can lead to a condition that has been labelled 'multiple personality'.

We all have subpersonalities: for example, a part of us that is wise, a part that is a mother or father, a part that loves to dance, a part that is sad. These seem to be common – almost anyone can identify a 'part' of themselves that performs in a particular way. However, someone who has a multiple personality, often as a result of a long or extreme experience of sexual abuse, seems actually to have many whole or partial personalities.

For people with multiple personalities the continuous presence, the part most of us recognize as 'I', with continuity of memory, rarely has control. The 'I' part cannot choose or even tell which personality, part or fragment of a personality will be present at any time, even when the person wakes in the morning. Sometimes they will not have any overview of the situation at all, no sense of 'I'. They can spend days, weeks, months or even years in a personality before moving out of it.

Most of us find safety of a sort in being able to split off when we are being abused. We go to another place in ourselves to find a kind of comfort. However, there is no comfort in having a multiple personality, and there is a lot of distress in being unable to move between personalities. There may be only partial communication between personalities, each with their own preferences, skills and memories, and possibly no communication at all.

Continuing Family Abuse

Unfortunately, the family relationships of many adult survivors carry on being abusive. The old expectations of us, and the demands of the abusive parents and relatives with their negative view of us, make it impossible for us to develop and to separate ourselves from our abusive family. This keeps us locked into old and negative patterns of behaviour, where we expect very little of and for ourselves. Learning how to feel good and to respect ourselves is one of the biggest battles for adult survivors.

When we do break free of the family's expectations of us, a trusted other person or a group of other survivors to help us see the situation through can make all the difference, because we need this kind of help and support. It can be difficult in situations where people in our lives remind us of past events to see that we are not in fact in any danger – other than the danger of old defences getting in the way of good new relationships, which may be confrontative or difficult but may also allow or even encourage us to grow.

For some, there is the fear of there being nothing behind our defences. We feel empty and that life has no meaning for us. In order to get over the abuse we need to embrace the fact that, as children, we were whole and lovely, and to realize that that part of us is still there inside us, needing to be taken care of, loved and reclaimed.

So let us end this chapter by recognizing two things: firstly, that childhood sexual abuse has only recently begun to be recognized as a common occurrence; and secondly, and much more importantly, that people are now less likely than they once were to see it as the victim's fault. Sadly, the victims of sexual abuse, whether children or adult survivors, have not always been treated kindly and with concern. Sexual abuse has only recently become an issue that can be talked about freely, without stigma for the survivor. Even in the recent past it has been seen as something that you don't talk about, that you feel ashamed of, or that you see as your fault. Up until recently, if you had been sexually abused, you or your family were seen as dirty, bad or inadequate. It was safer to keep quiet.

Even now there are people who will put you down for having been abused, or who do see it as your fault. It is of course wise to be cautious about who you share information about your experiences of sexual abuse with.

But it was not your fault and we feel that it's good to be as open as you feel able to be with people whom you feel you can trust to be understanding and supportive. As adults there may sometimes be ways that we can prevent a situation from happening, and there may also very well not be. That is a difficult judgement to make about adult behaviour. But the situation is very different for children. Sexual abuse is never the child's fault or responsibility.

In the next chapter, we will look at what happens in some families, and how abuse can go unrecognized and unconfronted.

3. Unhappy Families

Human interaction is complicated, and although there may be similarities, no two families are ever exactly alike. There are, however, some generalizations that we can make about families in which abuse takes place, and it is these common threads that we examine in the first part of this chapter. Later in the chapter we will present case histories of some of these unhappy families.

Whether it is abusive or not, the family remains most people's first experience of other people, and the relationships and behaviours that we experience and learn within that situation have a very profound effect on all the relationships that we make throughout our lives – especially on our relationship with ourselves.

The way the family operates and relates to the world remains our primary experience of relating to a society – whether this is by isolating ourselves and feeling different, or by being social. We are very largely influenced in our earliest and most formative years by the behaviours and attitudes that we learn within our family, which at that stage forms the world we live in. We take the relationships we form as very young children into ourselves and we internalize them. They become parts of ourselves, sub-personalities. As we grow up and leave our family, we still have these parts playing inside us to a greater or lesser degree.

Children in abusive families are exposed to confusing

interactions on a regular basis, and as children we are usually in no position to argue with the authority of adults. We experience the most formative and lasting stages of our growth within our family life. The child who is abused within a family is abused by the very people she or he depends on for existence. They are responsible for shaping her or his way of being in the world. Very small children are unable to separate themselves in any way from what is happening to them; what happens to them becomes their reality. Their experiences form the fabric of their inner lives, and the adults who take care of them are their whole world. The bad feelings of being violated and hurt affect all their subsequent feelings about themselves, along with their relationships and their own growth processes.

In an abusing family, abusive behaviour becomes a part of 'normal' family life. It is very difficult for the victim to separate out her or his own abuse from all the other strands of abuse happening within the family.

One feature of dysfunctional families is that it is not possible to escape from the roles that we are cast in within the family. The family members, following the behaviour of the parents, behave in certain ways towards each other. There is an investment in staying the same and in being inflexible. Family members are also generally expected to think of others before themselves, and not to focus on their own needs. Children who break the family rules and put themselves first are often called 'selfish' and 'self-centred'.

In families and extended family get-togethers, the people who make up the significant part of any child's world are all there for the abused child to see. Within the family, and outside it, abused children may see in other people reflections of those who have hurt them, and begin to feel a need to defend themselves against their projected fears.

Their world has become a very unsafe place and they find many ways of defending themselves against the frightening and invasive things that have happened to them.

As we have already said, children are unable to blame their parents when their behaviour makes them feel bad; rather, they tend to internalize the feeling of badness, feeling that somehow they themselves are in the wrong. They then have to live with this feeling that they are bad. They may feel very uncomfortable in larger family gatherings, and often other relatives are only too ready to reinforce the child's sense of being the bad child in a good family, or even a bad child from a bad family. In such family gatherings, the child can feel hopeless and completely convinced of his or her own badness, seeing it confirmed from every side.

Children are unable to separate themselves from the beliefs these adults seem to have about them. Unsupported, they will believe they must have been so bad as to deserve this treatment, and that the adults are right about them and they *are* bad. There is no escape for them: they have to stay in the family, they have no choice. Dysfunctional families very often have a family member who takes on this 'bad' role, and family attitudes towards this individual can remain for a lifetime, however they may be disguised or elaborated upon.

Some abused children can come to feel that they are special because of the way an adult is abusing their sexuality. They learn to ignore the whole of who they are and see themselves as only sexual objects. They may feel angry and powerless and seek to have some control in the situation by manipulating the person who is abusing them or by taking on a powerful central role in the family. These children are responding to being sexually abused by

51

exploiting their sexual power. They are doing their best in a bad situation. When we are confused in this way as children, we cannot escape from negative feelings such as shame and guilt. These feelings of shame and guilt underlie our whole sense of self-worth and adequacy and make it feel unsafe for us to be open, vulnerable or needy. We close down parts of ourselves in order to cope and to feel that we are in some way in control of the situation.

Distinguished writer and psychoanalyst Alice Miller talks of 'poisonous pedagogy' in her books, referring to the way in which children are denied rights and are seen as needing to be trained and controlled by parents. Violence is often seen as an accepted form of controlling children. Attitudes are instilled in children who in their turn become parents and practise this kind of parenting, condoning and justifying abusive behaviour towards children.

Such families are focused on adult expectations and adult needs and deny the importance of the feelings of a young child. The parents, out of touch with their own feelings, are unable to give their child healthy examples of bonding with others or relating successfully.

We don't have to think back very far to remember the prevalence of ideas about 'original sin', when children were seen as being born inherently bad and sinful. It was a particularly strongly held belief in Victorian times but it by no means ended with that era. Children's self-will is still often seen as something wicked and sinful that must be curbed at an early age. They are subject to similar violations from their parents that their parents were subject to in their own upbringing. Their parents believe that this is the right way for children to be brought up because they have experienced these attitudes and behaviours for all of their own lives since being small children themselves. Just as they may not have questioned their parents' behaviour towards them, and their entire method of parenting them, they do not question these deeply held beliefs now.

Implicit in this attitude is the expectation of the child's obedience and respect for her or his parents. It endorses all the adults' behaviours towards the child, however brutal that behaviour may be or however hurt the child may feel by the parents' behaviour. Because our parents are so important to us in our early years of life, we tend to believe that they are right in all that they do. Most children, even as adults, are never fully able to challenge the behaviour of their parents towards them, or even to question their method of parenting. They have come to accept it as the way children should be brought up, and they are deeply convinced that they must be respectful and grateful to their parents. Most of our parents were brought up with the belief that punishment is good for children, and that children are sinful, wicked and must be taught to be good. Cruel behaviour of all kinds can then be justified as a necessary part of parenting.

This gives rise to one of the most damaging features of early childhood abuse, which is that as children we have to suppress many of our earliest feelings. We are not able to address our feelings of anger and rage to those that hurt us at the time that it happens. Many children are brought up like this, afraid to express their anger at their parents, who during our childhood are usually physically much bigger than we are.

Since it is unsafe to show our feelings even to the people who are taking care of us, our world no longer feels safe. Suppressing feelings and keeping things inside becomes habitual, and this can lead to depression of parts of ourselves. It is not possible to close off early memories and feelings such as anger, shame or distress without affecting who we are as a person on many other levels. Inside and outside the family we will be changed in ways that can leave us vulnerable to further abuse, as we said in chapter two.

We need to be able to make a relationship with someone we can trust to listen to our feelings about what has happened to us, someone who does not judge us for our feelings or for our experiences. Unless we acknowledge and grieve the injustice of having our childhood robbed from us and of having been traumatized and violated as a child, we will not be able to begin the healing process fully.

Positive early learning experiences in relationships come from trusting people and feeling safe, and these healthy learning experiences are denied to abused children. Their abusing family determines the way in which they are likely to feel about themselves and their bodies, and affects how they relate to others, possibly for all of their lives.

There is a vast difference between what our culture accepts as the normal treatment of children and treatment that would be unacceptable to any reasonably assertive adult. Where adults may usually demand and expect fair treatment and to be listened to, in many families children cannot have the same expectation, and certainly not with any kind of consistency.

It's important to remember that appearances can be deceptive. Most of the people we talked to about their abuse had parents who were well-respected members of the community. They did not exhibit overly unnatural behaviours outside their family lives. In the climate of the time, their behaviour definitely did not give rise to active concern about the welfare of their children.

One significant reason why the abuse in these families went unnoticed and unconfronted is that abusing families are very often 'private'. There is a tendency for them to have few links to life outside the home. Other people may not be made welcome unless they collude with the abuse, either actively or passively.

Some of the distress in these unhappy families is clear from the following stories, which show how difficult it is for children who grow up in abusive families, and what effect being trapped in these families has on them as children and, later, as adults.

Gail's earliest memories are of helping her elderly next-door neighbours, as well as looking after her brothers and sisters. By caring for others so much she now feels that she was hoping someone would give *her* the caring and affection that was so lacking in her life as a child.

Both Gail and her elder sister Jean were physically and emotionally abused by their father over a period of ten years. He sexually abused Jean for the whole of that time, and directly sexually abused Gail for a six-month period.

Gail's father eventually became a bank manager, although for most of their childhood he was an angry and bitter man, constantly passed over for promotion. They were not well off, and he kept his family in an unnecessary state of poverty while he kept up his own appearances. He kept a very strict eye on the family, and they lived in a very isolated way, not interacting fully with the local community. His strict treatment of his children was endorsed by the cultural norms of the repressive society that he had been brought up in and was bringing his children up in.

He used to beat his wife frequently and, as his children grew older, he started to beat them instead. He was a violent man and the children lived in constant fear of his brutality. The sexual abuse began when Gail's sister Jean was nine and their mother was pregnant again.

Her father developed an obsession for Jean. He came to her bed at night and stood over her, ordering her to move over and make room for him beside her. Then he got in with her and began fondling and kissing her. Although his penis was not erect, he would get on top of her and go through the motions of sexual intercourse. Gail, lying in the bed next to her sister's, has no clear memory of what she saw or heard: she only knows what her sister has since told her.

On some level, though, Gail does seem to have known, as she began to be seductive with her father in order to get at least some attention. She now has painful memories of trying to get his attention in this seductive way. She had seen him being sexual with her elder sister, and she had seen him masturbating himself, so she clearly had the message that being sexual was the way to get his attention.

The children's clothes were kept in a wardrobe in their father's bedroom. This seems to have been so that he could have contact with the girls when they went to get their clothes, as he spent quite a lot of time at home lying on his bed. Sometimes when Gail went into the room to get her clothes from the wardrobe, she would act seductively, wanting his attention. She felt very frightened when this turned into her father fondling her and French kissing her and pushing his penis against her.

She is left with feelings of guilt and shame and a sense of having encouraged the situation, although at the time she felt as if she had no control over herself or the situation. For most of her life Gail has felt that she has been playing a game in order to survive. She feels that she has never really known who she is as a person.

For Gail's father, intelligence and educational prowess

were crucial. He valued Jean's intelligence and avidly followed her progress at school. Interestingly, Gail, an extremely intelligent and articulate person, somehow failed her eleven plus! From then on her father dismissed her as stupid and ignorant. Up to that time he had bullied her and hit her a lot. In ignoring her, he also stopped physically abusing and bullying her.

Since there was little connection with other families, and no one to report what was happening to social workers or the police, no one ever intervened in the situation to help Gail or her sister. Instead, their father's possessiveness towards her sister culminated in a terrible and violent scene, which Gail saw.

Angry that Jean had been talking to someone at work, their father lost his temper completely and began to hit her violently. Fearing that her sister would be killed, Gail rushed out and got the police. The police came and took Jean to the police station where she was questioned as to whether her father had had intercourse with her. Although she was then 19, Jean had never been allowed to have any friends, and had never spoken to anyone about sex. Sex had also never been talked about in the family, so Jean was relatively uninformed. She therefore naively believed that her father had in fact had intercourse with her, so that, when he asked her, she told the police doctor that, yes, her father had had intercourse with her. She was examined by the doctor and he found she was still a virgin. From then on he dismissed everything Gail and Jean said as lies.

Their father never admitted the truth of the abuse, and Jean was taken away, with a great deal of secrecy, to stay with some 'family friends' in the country. She was then sent to a psychiatric hospital and she never returned to the family home. The blame was put squarely on Jean and her problems, and no one believed that their father was at fault in any way.

It seems that at this point the children's mother finally told their father to stop masturbating in front of the family. Prior to that, he would sit with his feet up on the television in their small parlour with the family all sitting quietly around him, and, taking his penis out, he would masturbate himself openly. This went on for some years.

Gail left home as soon as she could. She had spent years helping her mother with the housework and listening to her troubles. When her mother felt tired, which she very often did, Gail did the family chores. Having therefore always considered herself her mother's helper and confidante, she was shocked when her mother's attitude completely changed towards her after she left home. It was as if what she had considered to be a special friendship when she lived at home had never existed.

Gail was left with a chronic fear of men, as was her sister Jean.

Although Gail forgot about her abuse until a long time after she left home, she subsequently sought help and eventually went into long-term psychotherapy with Rex, with whom she was able to develop a trusting relationship. In her two years of therapy, as her memories of the abuse began to surface, she explored some of the painful and distressing situations that had occurred in her childhood. She was able to express her anger and pain at what had happened to her and to her sister, and to look at the effects it had had on all the family members.

Her sister has never been able to talk about her terrifying experiences or to work therapeutically on her problems. Despite this, she has worked as a counsellor with victims of rape and abuse and has given interviews about the subject in the media.

It seems to be a frequent experience for children of large, abusive families to feel isolated from each other. They are generally unable to communicate fully or share painful feelings and memories when they are living within the family, and there is often a pretence of happy families, while deep feelings of insecurity and shame are buried beneath the surface. Family members are vulnerable to manipulation by their parents and by each other.

As the family members leave home the parents often cling to a fantasy that if the whole family gets along together, everything will be all right. They cherish the belief that their family life was once good and that in the past theirs was a happy family, having forgotten and denied their own abusive behaviour towards their children. Many adult children of abusive and dysfunctional families choose to go along with these beliefs rather than to challenge them. There often remains an enormous investment in their parents' attitude towards them, built on a foundation of uncertainty and insecurity.

Family gatherings can add to the pain and to the pretence. Many of the family members bring very difficult feelings, wondering how to relate to the other members of their family, and frictions often do occur. But so often the act is played out, each participant sitting on their feelings and taking a part in what may be a celebration, Christmas, a wedding or a funeral – and then it's time to go. Nothing is expressed or cleared. The bad feelings hang heavily and nothing is said. Each person is left to deal in their own way with the pain and denial and dishonesty.

Children in dysfunctional families are not able to make strong and healthy relationships with their parents. The relationships are frequently based on intimidation and a lack of clear communication, and the children are inhibited in their ability to challenge their parents in a healthy way. The powerful hold the parents maintain disables any of the children's attempts to level with them. They cannot speak about their difficulties in their relationships, or their feelings about their abusive pasts.

The family has to collude in a shared denial of the past traumas. There is a huge investment in keeping the lid on painful secrets, which are never allowed full expression. Family togetherness is then based on a distorted reality in which everyone has a separate memory of the past trauma that can never be mentioned. This collusive silence denies the reality of how bad things really have been, and so insecurity and fear take the place of communication and fact.

Within each child who has not been able to make a trusting relationship with their parents and whose needs have not been fully met, there is a terrible fear of abandonment and complete withdrawal of their parents' love. They will do almost anything to make sure that this does not happen. Because of their insecure upbringing and their inadequate parenting, resulting in low self-esteem, children from abusive and dysfunctional families are also unable to make close links with each other. They are unable to support each other while they are growing up within the family. Each of the children is suffering in his or her own way. Because of their unmet needs they are unable to meet the needs of their brothers and sisters. In a dysfunctional family, 'the others' can represent rivals for any kind of attention or affection from their parents.

Since the emotional life of the family is based on the suppression of painful and difficult feelings, there is often a scapegoat or problem child within the family where the conflicts and painful feelings are focused. In Gail's family that child was her sister Jean, who was also the child who suffered the most sexual abuse.

A woman whom we will call Eva was abused intermittently by her father from the age of nine until she was 12. Her father touched her breasts and kissed her, and fondled her genitals. When she was 12 she refused to let him come near her and she kept out of his way. It felt, she recalls, like turning away a boyfriend, and she experienced an awful feeling of confusion. She wanted him as her father, but he wanted sex from her, and that revolted her. She had to reject him, although she longed for a loving father.

Eva feels that when she rejected her father she lost both of her parents, since they were clearly supportive of each other. She felt that she couldn't go to either for confidential talks or for support. She could no longer expect proper parenting, and, in a disturbing way, she felt as if she was living with a divorced partner. She thought about leaving home, but she realized that she was too young.

Twenty-five years later, Eva still struggles with a deep sense of guilt and shame that she was aroused sexually by her father. There was some sense of pleasure in the sex and in the attention that she received, but it was not a pleasure she felt good about. Although Eva was not aware of it at the time, her father was also abusing her older sister.

Eva remembered her abuse after she left home to go to college. She felt isolated and suicidal, and it was then that she talked to her sister, who told her that she had been abused by their father too. It was very important to Eva to know that she had not been the only one, and that also helped her realize that she was not responsible for the abuse. She told her boyfriend, who now remembers her as having been very cold and distant about it at the time. This disclosure marked the time when she began to recover.

Eva feels very anxious about her ability to forget and her subsequent remembering. She worries that if she can forget so effectively, what else is there that she has forgotten and not yet remembered? She has a feeling of rootlessness and lack of trust and an uneasy sense of other things she does not yet know about.

Eva also has a very difficult and painful memory of what she feels was abuse of her younger brother. She was 14 at the time and he was very small, just two years old. He was a very attractive little boy who was doted on by the family. She remembers cuddling him, and feeling confused about her behaviour. Now she looks back and feels she 'went too far' with him, and that she was becoming abusive. Her brother, sensing that something was uncomfortable and wrong, became very uneasy and ran off. Eva rationalized it at the time by thinking that it wasn't very important or very bad.

She now feels bad about her behaviour. Although she wasn't aware of it at the time, she thinks that she wanted to humiliate her brother. She wanted a kind of revenge and to be somehow in a more powerful place than him. She finds that very frightening. It happened just once as far as she knows, and she still carries a sense of guilt about it.

Her older brother Tony later abused his own daughter. When the family found out about it they went into a tremendous state of shock, and after that there were many family discussions about all the abuse that had gone on within the family over the years. Eva recalls her older brother Tony's sexual 'experimentation' with herself, which was very abusive. She recalls how similar in some ways the experience was to being abused by her father. One difference is that she feels that she could have said no to her brother; nothing like so much was at stake as when she said no to her father. She was taken aback by the similarity between her brother's and her father's actions, and thought that somehow her brother must have witnessed their father's abuse of her, even though she knows he could not have. Tony, however, justifies his abusive behaviour as 'just growing up' and 'not serious', and feels that Eva was as much to blame.

After the abuse, Eva was left with feelings of very low self-esteem. She feels that the abuse she experienced in her childhood has had a deep and pervasive effect on her throughout her life. She has had great difficulty trusting anybody at all, particularly men.

When she did eventually confront her father with his abuse of her, Eva's father would only say, 'I've said I'm sorry, what else can I do?', leaving Eva to feel that it was her problem and her responsibility. Both of her parents are afraid of the consequences of doing something about themselves such as going to therapy. They are not able even to accept between themselves the enormous amount of suffering and distress that was caused and which is still being felt. Sexual abuse can never be seen as something that just happened 10, 20, 30 or more years ago. Its effects last throughout our lives. But we can get help and learn to deal with the pain and to live with the memories.

When her father was abusing her, Eva felt that it wasn't herself particularly that he really wanted. She felt that it wasn't important to him who she was; she could have been anybody. She felt unseen, and still feels that people don't see her – that they see her as a symbol. The feeling of there being nothing behind our defences is a common fear for people who have been abused.

Children idealize their parents and need to believe that they are perfect. Unable to believe that their parents are bad, they take the blame on themselves. They are left with feelings of guilt and shame which become internalized and contribute to their feelings of low self-esteem. These feelings can manifest in self-abuse. Eva tried to scar herself to make herself unattractive. She had negative associations with being found attractive, which got her attention but in a way that felt bad and confusing. Abused children often try to scar themselves as if to confirm their sense of being worthless and of being valued only for their bodies. They feel they are only objects, to be exploited by others in a way that leaves them deeply hurt and internally scarred.

Eva very often wished that her mother would die and that she would have to run the house and look after everyone. Many children who experience their parents as out of control take on the role of the adult and caretaker in order to keep themselves feeling safe as children. They go on as adults to maintain a deep need to be in control of every aspect of their lives, particularly in relationships. Eva dealt with her painful feelings by focusing her attention on her schoolwork during her childhood and she did very well academically.

In Eva's family the parents took very traditional roles. Her father was dominant and exerted a lot of power in the family. The children were expected to do what they were told. Their mother endorsed this and threatened the children by warning them that she would tell their father when he got home. In this kind of family none of the children can learn to express themselves in a healthy way, and they are especially not able to express their negative feelings. A very dominating father does not allow children any sense or expression of themselves. The effects on the family and feelings of the individuals within the family are repressive. Eva and her siblings were additionally confused because, although their father had high expectations of them, he gave them a double message. The underlying message was, 'Don't do any better than I'm doing.' Their mother let them know that she didn't like success. It isn't surprising that, except for Eva, the family grew up to be underachievers.

Sally was abused by her grandfather at a very young age. This early sexual awareness caused her a lot of pain and feelings of shame. She felt different from other children and somehow bad. As a small child she taught the little girl who lived near their new home that it felt good to press down on a full bladder, just above her pubic bone. The little girl was not allowed to talk to Sally again and Sally was left with a deep sense of shame and of being bad. Sally also remembers playing with the little boys in the field behind their house and being ostracized by all the local girls as being 'nasty and dirty' for playing 'Show me yours and I'll show you mine'.

Every so often the family would go and stay with the paternal grandparents. Sally was frightened of her grandfather and did not enjoy these visits. She never trusted him or felt safe with him, even when he was nice to her. He enjoyed terrifying children with unpleasant 'games' which had a vicious and persecutory edge to them, and yet her grandmother would encourage Sally to go to him in the garden shed, and it was there that he abused her. The other place that he abused her was in her bedroom. Her grandfather would order all the family to bed after lunch. Sally still remembers the sound of the door handle rattling as he came into her room. He would read to her from the Bible and then tickle her, and it always ended in his patting her over her vulva. It was pleasurable for Sally and yet she knew it was a bad thing for him to do, although she could not express this as a small child.

It was not until she was in her mid-teens that she was able to refuse to go and stay with her grandfather. In her therapy, during her mid-thirties, she felt ashamed even telling her therapist what had happened. She was particularly ashamed of the pleasurable feelings that she had felt when her grandfather touched her vulva. Even now she feels that she doesn't know deep down what are acceptable feelings of pleasure and touch. She has a constant sense of confusion and shame around her feelings of excitement and sexual arousal.

Sally's father died when she was seven and even before that he had been absent for most of her childhood. On the occasions when he was at home, he was very unpredictable, either 'blowing his top' or 'larking about'. So Sally's relationship with her brother Sam was always very important to her; she always felt, however, that she could never be good enough or clever enough for him. Although she tried very hard to please him, nothing she did ever seemed to be enough for Sam.

When their father died, their grandfather told Sam, who was then ten and a half years old, that he was the man in the family now. When Sally was nine, Sam started going to boarding school and when he came back in the holidays he was sexual with Sally in the family living-room. He was fascinated by her body and wanted her to show him her vagina, and to show her his penis. This led to them almost having penetrative sex, and Sally remembers a feeling of wanting her brother to penetrate her. She found their sexual play and his attention to her very exciting and very pleasurable.

Her mother realized that something was going on and gave Sally, just nine years old, a book to read about sex. She doesn't know if her brother was spoken to about the situation, but somehow Sally felt that she was seen as having been in some way responsible for what was happening.

She often saw her mother embracing her brother very closely and it seemed to her that they were rubbing up against each other. Sally felt lonely and excluded. She also felt dismissed, invisible and unimportant. She felt very isolated, and this affected her life for many years when she carried the feeling of having to cope alone and do everything by herself.

For many years Sally was unable to make close friendships. She had many abusive encounters with men, and she did not form good relationships. She did not know how to protect herself as she was so low in self-esteem. Although she had very bad feelings about her sexuality and a terrible sense of shame, which came from her childhood abuse, she saw herself as attractive only sexually and not in any other way, and she became very sexually available to men. Having felt deeply distrustful of her grandfather, her mother and her brother for most of her life, she doesn't find it easy to trust others enough to believe that she can have an intimate relationship with someone and that it will be safe.

Since she has looked at her abuse over several years of therapy, in both individual therapy and group work, Sally has been able to acknowledge it fully for the violation that it was and for the damage it has caused her. She has gradually learnt to value herself. Her relationships have become loving and strong, and she has been able to form good friendships with men. She worked for several years with a woman therapist and has, over the last year, worked with a man, which she has found very helpful. With him she has explored her earliest childhood and the treatment she suffered then.

Dora was 34 and chronically low in self-esteem when she first went to see a therapist. She had what the therapist called 'bio-energetics', which involved her lying on a couch with her eyes closed, while he, wearing tight red velvet trousers, would stand leaning against the couch, sometimes rubbing his penis against her. She was shocked by this behaviour. Unable to deal with it in any way, she almost disbelieved her own experience, so that despite this man's abusive treatment of her, she went to him for four sessions. Some very old memories were evoked for her during this time.

One of these memories was of herself as a very small child, perhaps two years old or, at most, three. She was in her parents' bedroom in the morning and her mother had got up to prepare breakfast. She had a clear memory of her father exposing himself to her, and was aware that this had happened on several occasions. She remembers looking at his penis as if it were something very familiar to her. Then, the last time it happened, her father, seeing her looking, became very angry with her. She felt bewildered and that she had somehow been very bad. He continued to be very unpleasant and rejecting towards her, although she tried hard to be 'daddy's little friend' again.

Dora's parents were religious and authoritarian and very strict with their five children. They also had high academic expectations of them. Dora recalls, as a small child, looking at her brothers and sisters and wondering how it was that they were so naturally good. She felt that she had been born bad. Dora failed academically and was unable to make lasting friendships. She felt deeply inadequate and also had a very poor body image. From an early age she became involved with unpleasant and abusive men with whom she did not form any kind of bonding or lasting relationships.

Her older brother developed an incestuous fascination for her. When she was a young teenager he would follow her into their garden and grope at her breasts, and try to feel her up. She felt very frightened of him. Hating her developing body, she felt numbed to the changes that were taking place in herself. Her mother, who idealized the males in the family, noticed Dora's brother's lustful attitude towards her, and said things to Dora which implied that she was lucky to be receiving that kind of attention.

Dora still struggles with a very early, pre-verbal memory, which dates back to her very early childhood, perhaps when she was a baby, and which involves a man's penis, but she has not yet got a clear memory of this. She had a fear of men's penises for many years, even as an adult.

She also had strongly ambivalent feelings about men, both a deep fear of and a fascination with them. She felt very inadequate in her relationships with men and behaved either in a naïve and childlike way or in a rejecting way. For many years she wasn't able to sustain intimate relationships, and had only short-lived and abusive sexual relationships with men. She easily felt invisible and that she didn't count. She could become angry in a way that felt out of control and destroy the links that she had made. She could be critical and persecutory and isolate herself by behaving in this way.

A turning-point occurred for her when she went to a

workshop for incest survivors. She felt that it might relate to her in some way, but she did not allow herself to feel that anything 'very serious' had happened to her, and did not count her experiences as having been 'sexual abuse'.

When she finished the workshop, she felt almost able to say that she had been abused, and today – some years later – she is finally able to say, 'I was abused as a child.' It has taken her until well into her forties to be able to own this, and she still has to affirm the truth of it to herself each time she talks about it. She finds herself realizing yet again that her experiences clearly were sexual abuse, and were very damaging to her, and yet even now a part of her denies this. There is still an absolute denial of abuse of any kind in the family.

So many people suffer from a denial of their abuse. They minimize it, maybe saying, 'It was only touching (or flashing, or looking) – it wasn't really that abusive.' Unless we fully acknowledge our experiences of abuse, we don't allow ourselves to be in touch with the feelings of pain and confusion that we felt as children, and the healing process is blocked.

Margaret is the youngest child of a family of three children. Her sister is close to her in age, and her brother is 10 years older than she is. Academic achievements were considered more important for boys by her father and, at six years old, her brother was sent off to boarding school. Her brother was the favoured child and was treated specially when he came home for his holidays. Margaret has memories of herself and her sister being treated 'like servants' in comparison, as if they were insignificant.

Margaret's father had sexual affairs with his secretaries throughout her childhood. They were always many years younger than he was. Her mother spent a lot of time alone at home feeling depressed and resentful and complaining that her husband had made her life a misery. She had a martyred stance and played out a victim role, to which he played the big bully. She forgave him his 'misdemeanours', but she never let him forget them.

Margaret's father was very authoritarian within the family and although her mother took a lesser role, she criticized him behind his back continually. Margaret discovered that the only way to have intimate contact with her mother, and to feel at all close to her, was to take part in these 'bitchy' conversations. She also remembers that her father often hit her. He would lash out at her, and she was constantly afraid of his violence.

Margaret now remembers that she was first abused when she was a baby. She was abused then by her grandfather, whom she now believes also abused her mother. She clearly remembered her own abuse recently during a group therapy session when the participants were doing an exercise in which they were reparenting each other. Margaret was evoking her memories and feelings of being a baby when she suddenly had a disturbing memory around her mouth. She later recovered a clear memory of her grandfather putting his penis into her mouth.

This was the first memory Margaret had of this abuse. She had been working in therapy on her experiences of abuse for some years before that.

The first memory Margaret recaptured of her childhood sexual abuse was of her father taking nude photographs of her when she was five years old, having coerced her into taking off her clothes. It felt bad to Margaret, but she so very much wanted to please him. He kept telling her how good she was and how well she was doing when she took off first

71

her jumper and then the rest of her clothes. She remembers her mother coming out and saying angrily to her father that she had had enough of his behaviour and that she wasn't going to stand for any more of it. Nothing comforting was said to the small child, who was shivering without her clothes on. She was just told brusquely to put her clothes on again and was left feeling that somehow she had done something horribly wrong.

Margaret was 34 when she had that memory, and she had just started to see a therapist. She had sought therapy because, when she became involved in relationships with men, she found that she was consistently terrified of their getting angry with her. Six weeks after her first therapy session she had that first clear memory of having been abused. She spoke about it to her sister, who was three years older than she was, and her sister remembered someone talking about it. Margaret recalls feeling extremely relieved. She had a witness and she knew that it was true and that it really did happen. Her fear was that she had made it up somehow. This is a fear that lurks behind all her subsequent memories, even though she is now clear about their reality.

Two and a half years later she had a memory of anal abuse, and with this memory came images of her brother. She could feel the pain in her body and she would see her brother's face along with the body memory, but somehow separate. Again she asked her sister if she knew anything, and this time her sister became angry. She talked about a strange boy who had lived up the road, and denied any memories of abuse within their family. She said that these things were best left in the past and that Margaret was only upsetting herself by 'digging them up'. Margaret's friends of that time said the same things to her, and so at that time she convinced herself that these things were indeed best left alone.

Her sister did remember an incident when some boys they met locally wanted to put their hands in the girls' knickers. She said that they hadn't let them, but Margaret knew that they had. She realized that, being the elder, her sister had felt somehow responsible for her and guilty.

She remembers watching a programme on television about child sexual abuse, and recalls that it was the first time she could feel really angry with the perpetrator. She still, however, saw the little girl who had been abused as bad. Margaret had internalized her own feelings of 'badness' and she identified with the little girl. She remembers thinking, 'There's something bad about you', about the little girl, and therefore she felt that the little girl had somehow deserved the abuse.

As an adult too, Margaret had always felt that she was bad and feared that there was something about her that led men to behave badly towards her in relationships. She felt that she must bring out the worst in them. She didn't realize that she was drawn to abusive men because that had been her experience of significant male figures in her life.

Margaret's mother was unable to be a warm, caring, or physically available mother to any of her children. She had to go into hospital to have Margaret when her sister was three and Margaret sometimes wonders if her father, who abused Margaret throughout her childhood, also abused her sister then.

Margaret remembers both her sister and her elder brother being very aggressive with her. There was so little love and affection of any form within the family and certainly no model of kind and loving people for the children to learn from.

Margaret recently had a memory of her father abusing her orally when her brother was in the room. She was about three at the time and her brother was 13. It was shortly after this that her brother began to abuse her anally when she came home from school for his holidays.

During a one-year psychotherapy course two years ago, she dreamt that she was bleeding from her vagina and that a woman packed her with paper. She rang her mother to talk to her about it and her mother changed the subject quickly. Margaret then decided to go and see a hypnotherapist and counsellor, and it was then that she realized the appalling extent of her experiences as a child.

She had a memory of her brother scratching her around her vagina. She remembers him running a little wooden car up and down over her vulva and then shoving a wooden toy soldier inside her. She must then have passed out because the next thing she remembers is being carried downstairs by her parents and put onto the dining-room table. She remembers a lot of rustling and her mother putting something around her vagina. She remembers seeming to be outside her body and feeling very peaceful.

She woke up later in bed in the nursery and recalls the lovely feeling of clean sheets and the sun streaming in through the window, and then other feelings came. She felt that there was no escape, that she just wanted to die. She remembers her heavy sighs and thinking that nothing had changed. It was going to go on and on: 'Rupert does it when he's home from boarding school and, when he goes back, there's daddy.' She thinks that she somehow disassociated herself from her body in order to be able to survive.

She has no clear memory of when it all stopped, but when she was 10 she spoke to her mother about all the blood and 'funny stuff' she saw in the toilet when she used it. It was, Margaret recalls, as if she had let herself see it for the first time, even though it had been going on for a long time. There had also been blood and 'white stuff' on her nightie. Her mother had never mentioned this to her, but she now took Margaret to the doctor and Margaret heard the doctor talk to her mother about a fissure. She felt very special and important. There was something serious happening to her – she might even die. She remembers that after that there was no more blood in the toilet. She felt a little disappointed – she was not dying, life would be 'ordinary'. She had experienced attention when she was abused and she felt insignificant and of little value otherwise.

Margaret's father was dead by the time she recovered her memories, and her mother refuses to have any kind of conversation on the subject.

In this atmosphere of physical and sexual abuse, the children effectively carry on abusing one another; there is no refuge or place of safety in this kind of family. Each child has to look out for her or himself, and they cannot support each other. The children grow up feeling that there will be nothing for them unless they fight for it.

In spite of all this, the sense of obligation towards our parents lives on, and many survivors suffer from feelings of guilt when they are trying to work out the truth about what happened to them in their childhood. It is as if we have now become responsible for their parents' feelings. The irony of this is that their parents denied them *their* feelings as children, and probably still do now that they are adults.

It is a huge step to confront your parents; your past is so

bound up with them and they have had such a strong control over you. In abusing families this control can be especially binding as the child victim of abuse is robbed of feelings of esteem and self-worth, so necessary for children as they grow up in order for them to be able to separate themselves successfully from their parents and live healthy adult lives.

In most families there is a strong ethos of 'forgive and forget' and 'leave the past well alone'. Experiences that have been awful and very damaging to a young child are minimized and considered 'best forgotten'. People who do explore and work on their abusive childhoods are often treated with anger and resentment by other family members, who are threatened by the possibility of having to deal with painful memories that they have suppressed. It is often the case that adult families function on a sort of status quo, an unspoken 'agreement' not to address the past. Painful memories are not welcomed and there is no way of acknowledging or addressing them.

Difficult feelings, such as resentment for not having been the one chosen for 'special' attention, or guilt for not having been able to protect the victim of abuse, or even feelings about having been part of the abusing behaviour, can be stirred and many people choose not to look at these feelings. Family members who have not acknowledged their own childhood feelings of pain and rage often feel angry towards those that do. They minimize the experiences that their brothers or sisters are working through, feeling that if they themselves can just live with it and get on with their lives, their siblings ought to be able to do so as well.

The person who is working on him or herself often becomes unacceptable to those who are suppressing their past memories and not wishing to explore them. Again they may experience feelings of isolation and of being punished in some way or ostracized by other family members. It takes a lot of courage to decide to stand up for the small child within ourselves, and to reclaim the feelings that were never allowed in the past.

Often parents have mellowed to some extent with age and it can be hard to face frail and elderly people with their actions of 30, 40 or even 50 years ago. It may be that this is not the best thing to do anyway. That's a decision that each of us must make for ourselves.

We recognize that it is very rare for people who have been abused to work through their feelings about the abuse within their family of origin. Most of us need help from outside. We may get this kind of support from friends, or we may need to go and look for it from others who have experienced abuse and worked through it for themselves. We may also need help from professionals, and we go on to look at this process in the next chapter.

4. Going for Help

There is a growing awareness among survivors and those who work with them of how deeply we are affected by the anguish and terror that go with being sexually abused as a child. The shocked state that we may go into is almost hypnotic, and this means that the trauma and the defences are deep. The fact is that we are unable to understand what is happening to us when we are children. Even if we did 'know' intellectually what was happening to us, we still would not be able to understand why these people were doing this to us. As children we can only defend ourselves against an abusive situation and the feelings that it brings up in us by closing down part of ourselves and staying that way. This 'closing down' happens on a very deep level and becomes a part of who we are. We cannot think of being someone other than who we are, complete with our defences; they are so much a part of us, we don't even know that they are there. So going for help is important. We need others to recognize when we are being defensive and to point it out to us, and someone to support us in working through our difficult feelings.

Being in individual therapy with a therapist who understands the significance of having been sexually abused as a child may sometimes be difficult, but is a very rewarding experience. To have someone there to listen to you and support you in an ongoing way is invaluable. As things come up in your therapy week by week they can be acknowledged and worked through. A therapist who has experience of working with people who have been sexually abused can ask the right questions of you when you are stuck, and give you good prompting. A good therapist will help you to uncover the details of the abuse and to look at how you coped with it, and how those coping behaviours affect you in your life now.

A group where you can work with other survivors is another way of working on yourself that has great value. The fact that you are in a group with others who have been abused means there can be a level of support and understanding that can make you feel as if you belong somewhere for the first time in your life, rather than feeling like an isolate or an outcast. Where else could you find a 'replacement' for a family that disbelieves and rejects you, and feel so believed, acknowledged and supported!

PROFESSIONAL ABUSE

Before we describe the process of psychotherapy in more depth, we want to sound some warning bells about the pitfalls of going for professional help. Sadly, when a person who has been sexually abused considers going for help with the problems that we have described in earlier chapters, one of the issues that she or he has to be careful of is a possibility of further abuse – this time by professionals. Some people in the helping professions are lonely, inadequate, or sexually opportunistic, and many therapists have been known to abuse their clients.

Helping or Harming?

The whole issue of 'helping' someone in therapy needs to be considered carefully. We are aware that 'helping' puts the therapist in a position of power and can leave the client with less power. In order for therapy to work well, a therapist shouldn't do anything for anyone that that person can do for themselves. A good therapist will help you just as much as you really need, and no more.

It's tempting for the therapist to want to give the client constant feedback about what they think is or was happening to them. In fact, it's better for the client to find out for themselves what their issues are and what they need to do about them. The client will very often know the answer, and it is much better for them if they do find it for themselves rather than be given it. Sometimes the client *will* need help: it is a balance between giving the person room to grow, and not withholding from them the help that they need.

Unfortunately, some therapists enjoy the power they feel when they work with people, and are reluctant to let go of the feeling of being in control. If you feel that you are allowed by your therapist only to be needy and helpless during your sessions, then you should be able to talk to your therapist about it. You should get a sense from the therapist that they understand and recognize the issue of your own personal choice and power. Your therapist or counsellor should be willing to look at the way they are working with you and, if necessary, be prepared to make changes.

Boundaries and Responsibilities

Many survivors of sexual abuse have naturally become very suspicious and defensive, as part of their way of surviving abusive situations. Although this has worked well for them in the past, there is a cost for them in terms of their ability to make and maintain their relationships with others. When they recognize this, they may go to a therapist for help.

In therapy sessions the therapist has the same kind of duty to the client as an adult has to a child in terms of keeping the sexual boundaries clear. Unfortunately, some professionals disregard their responsibility in this area in the same way that some caretakers of children do.

Some therapists depend emotionally on the client for approval or affirmation, or for a loving or a sexual relationship. That would create a situation where the 'child' (client) is parenting the 'parent' (therapist). Since this happens so often to children who are sexually abused, you can see how disabling and unhelpful a further experience of an unsound relationship like this would be.

If the relationship between the therapist and the client involves a sexual relationship, the effect is virtually further childhood sexual abuse. The client brings their childlike part to the relationship, and is then abused.

Often the person going for help is already very vulnerable to being abused, especially the client who has positive feelings about their therapist and the therapy. They really want therapy to work for them, and they bring their best efforts and total belief in the therapist to the therapy situation. Because of their history, and their great need for acceptance and approval, the relationship begins with a lot of emotional charge. As in childhood, the need for acceptance and the goodwill the client brings into the relationship means that they will try all the time to give the therapist what he or she wants.

Usually, the client who was abused as a child lacks self-esteem, and that can make it very difficult for them to recognize clearly that they are being abused again. Being sexually abused by your therapist will bring about further undermining of your self-esteem, and compound any sense of low self-worth. The client's view of themselves as only a sexual object will be reinforced. They will continue to see themselves as having no intrinsic value as a person, which is the legacy for many people who have been sexually abused as children.

In all therapy the process of reparenting goes on in the therapeutic relationship, and, as we have said, therapists have the same duty as all parents do to their children to keep the boundaries clear. Even the thought or wish to have a sexual relationship with a client needs to be looked at and worked on in the therapist's supervision. So check out if the therapist you want to work with is in supervision. If a therapist is not in ongoing supervision, we think you shouldn't work with them. Every therapist needs supervision. If they tell you they don't need it, we advise you not to work with them.

The contract between the therapist and the client must be clear. The client is often paying the therapist handsomely to have a therapeutic relationship with them. There should be no dependent behaviour on the part of the therapist, and no amorous or sexual complications. The client should have the safety and protection from abuse that every professional should provide.

This reality is recognized by almost all professional organizations, which forbid professionals to have sexual relationships with clients. It is against the law in an increasing number of states in America for a professional to have sexual relations with a client, and, as far as we are concerned, that should be true everywhere.

In California it is a rule of law that every new client should be given a copy of a state-prepared booklet, 'Professional Therapy Never Includes Sex', which sets out the whole issue of professional sexual abuse in a very clear way. It says:

Therapists who encourage, ask for, or permit sexual involvement with their clients are exploiting them. Professional therapy never includes sex . . . All therapists are trained and educated to know that this kind of behavior is unethical, against the law, and can be harmful to the client.

It is *never* all right for your therapist or counsellor to have any kind of sexual relationship with you. It is also the therapist's responsibility to seek help for themselves if they are tempted to begin an inappropriate relationship with their client.

If you like your therapist and feel that you have worked well together, and that person begins to expect something from you personally, whether it is emotional or sexual, you should be able to talk to them directly about your feelings and get a good resolution for yourself. If you are not satisfied, then you can get in touch with the therapist's supervisor and make a complaint to them. If you do not get any satisfactory response from either the therapist or their supervisor, then you can report their behaviour to their professional association.

It is not a good idea to just let go of the therapy relationship and to find yourself another therapist without going through this process. Ideally, you will get help and support either to sort out the working relationship, or else with moving on to another therapist. Hopefully this would include special sessions to work through the change.

Once again, if you get into a situation like this, it isn't your fault. The therapist is the one who has responsibility for the situation, just as it is always the responsibility of the adult who should be parenting the child, to protect the child.

Sexual abuse by professionals seems to be a particularly difficult situation for men, as they are not used to seeing themselves as victims. They expect to see themselves as the person who is looking out for a sexual relationship, whether they are successful or not. They may feel more guilt and shame if they are not used to acknowledging their feelings and expressing them. They may be used to withholding how they really feel from others, and denying their pain.

Rex has worked with several male clients who had been sexually abused by female therapists from different schools of therapy. Two of those clients were so traumatized by what had happened to them that they were unwilling to have any details of their experiences mentioned in this book, as they were fearful of some further abuse on the part of their former therapists.

Each client was encouraged to have a sexual relationship with their therapist while carrying on having therapy with them. This means, in effect, that the client was being charged for having a sexual relationship with a therapist, while the therapist maintained themselves in a position of power. Certainly, once the therapist begins a sexual relationship with a client, true therapy ceases. The relationship becomes a confusing and negative power-game.

One client at least thought he should see the therapist's behaviour as a compliment, and he also felt responsible for it. The therapist carried on working with him weekly, and carried on charging him at the end of each session. It seems to us quite remarkable that she felt able to carry on in this way, and to rationalize charging him for an abusive situation that had quite clearly become undermining and counter-productive. She seems to have seen all the problems in the therapy as the client's problem, and not to have considered her own effect on him.

It is easy to say of any abused person that they should have left an abusive situation earlier, and important to remember that that kind of dependence is often what the person goes to the therapist for in the first place. The client needs to build up a trusting dependency relationship and to feel safe, so it's important not to blame the client and say that they shouldn't have let it happen. The responsibility for any professional abuse lies with the professional, just as the responsibility for all childhood sexual abuse lies with the adult who perpetrates it.

Because of the caution they may have learnt from their experience of having been sexually abused, some clients will not immediately be vulnerable to someone who is likely to be sexually abusive. They will make their own reserved kind of relationship with their therapist, and become vulnerable only as they begin to open up and trust the therapist. If the therapist is unprofessional and open to having sexual relationships with their clients, the possibility of abuse will then arise.

FINDING THE RIGHT THERAPIST

Although we have pointed out the difficulties of finding the right therapist for yourself, we think it's well worth the effort, as individual therapy for adult survivors of childhood sexual abuse can be one of the most effective ways to begin the process of recovery. Apart from the actual work, having someone who is there for you alone (at least, for an hour a week) is a very supportive experience and will help with your self esteem and encourage you to stay focused on the important issues that you need to work through.

The best way to find a therapist is through the personal recommendation of someone that you know who has worked with them. The fact is, though, someone else's choice may simply not be right for you, so you could still shop around.

When you look around for someone to work with, the style or type of therapy that you choose is actually not as important as the relationship between the client and the therapist. Bio-energetics, Gestalt, bodywork, existential psychotherapy, analysis – at the end of the day all these are ways of working. The work is the same in all cases: to uncover what has gone before and the deeply held feelings that go with it, and to help the person to work through those feelings. The technique is secondary to your feelings about the therapist or counsellor. It is vital that you feel comfortable and safe with her or him.

We recommend that you go to a number of therapists. Tell them that you are shopping around, that you want to ask lots of questions at the beginning of therapy, that you will be checking out other therapists, and that you would like to feel free to go away and think about it after the first session.

As a child, there were all those times when you couldn't or didn't dare ask about what was happening, when you couldn't check it out, or try a relationship for yourself before you committed yourself to it. This is your opportunity to make up for all the times that you couldn't check things out properly or get a straight answer when you were small, so pluck up your courage and go ahead and ask! As most therapists are self-employed, most will charge for a first session, but getting a good therapist, whom you will be sharing your self with, is worth taking time over.

Remember that you have a right to ask lots of questions at the beginning. You can ask questions like

- what is their experience of working with people who have been sexually abused as children?
- what do they feel about it in terms of its effect on the adult?
- do they see it as important?

A surprising number of therapists give only a passing look at sexual abuse in childhood, and do not recognize the need to work through the feelings that are left behind when we are assaulted in that way.

You can also ask your therapist how they see ending therapy, and when it would be – not perhaps in terms of time, as that is very difficult to estimate, but in terms of how they see a client as ready to leave therapy.

There may be more questions that you want to ask a prospective therapist. Don't hesitate to make a list and take it into the first session with you. A good therapist will appreciate the sense in what you are trying to do in making the list and asking the questions.

Working with Feelings

A history of having been sexually abused as a child is a fundamental issue. Work that is done in therapy which does not relate to that history will be shallow and insubstantial unless the feelings around the abuse are worked through.

It is vital for the therapist to recognize that the way the client behaves in their sessions is a true reflection of how that client is likely to interact in the world outside the therapy room. Just the same relationship can develop as if the therapist were a parent who must be pleased. Ideally, the therapist will be watchful not to allow the person to bring only their positive and adaptive feelings into the relationship in this way.

Every person, adult or child, has a full range of emotions and their reactions to those emotions within them. Fear, love, anger, grief, sadness and joy are the basic emotions to consider and work with. Envy and jealousy are powerful reactions to the basic emotions, which must also be acknowledged and dealt with as a part of any whole person.

Some of these emotions can obviously be painful to experience and deal with, and are easily ignored by clients, and even by therapists. It is very easy for a therapist and client to collude with one another in avoiding working with emotions that they may *both* find painful or distasteful. Often the client wants to avoid getting into painful feelings, and any cue from the therapist can easily be seen as 'permission' not to have to. There can be a great sense of relief for both the client and the therapist – the client thinking 'My therapist thinks I don't need to go into these feelings', and the therapist thinking 'She obviously doesn't need to go into these heavy feelings; she seems to have dealt with them well.'

Some therapists are afraid of their own anger, and therefore afraid of letting their clients get into their anger. There are therapists who are unsettled or even disgusted by the sight of an adult person getting in touch with, and loudly expressing, all the hurt, rage and despair that come from having been abused as a child. Any therapist who has not worked through their own anger about their childhood will have a resistance to encouraging their clients to express their own deep feelings around the issue.

The client will need to express the neediness, disappointment, anger and tears that are part of their history. It is vital that the therapist is able both to allow and to encourage the expression of all those feelings. Those feelings can and will be worked through. That process may take quite a while, and the angry feelings may go away for a while and then resurface. This is a natural part of the therapy process. We need to carry on with our expression of the hurt child within us whenever the need arises. You may feel so guilty and responsible for what happened that you are denying the reality that you were a child and it was not your fault. We sometimes need an advocate who will say 'That was not your fault', perhaps many times, until we can understand that and see that it is true.

If the client brings along a positive attitude, and perhaps works only on their sadness around their abuse and not their anger, there will still be some benefit, but they will be denying their powerful, angry and assertive emotions. This will mean they carry on in life with some of their ability to stand up for themselves still repressed.

At the other end of the spectrum a client who is only angry and critical, and cannot or will not explore and express their more tender emotions, will be unlikely to make positive relationships. A therapist should be willing and able to pick up on avoidance of intimacy, and to help the client who cannot or will not express all their emotions and acknowledge their need for relationships with others. Most clients who have been abused need help in expressing their love, joy and sadness, as well as their anger.

Dependence and Independence

The relationship between you as a client and your therapist needs to be good. You should feel they are 'on your side', and this will include a level of dependence on the therapist as the relationship develops. There is a real need here for a balance between dependence and independence. True independence is knowing when you need help and being able to ask for it. Co-dependence, on the other hand, means that you rely on others to define you, and that you are not recognizing what you feel, or what your own real choices are.

Many people who have been sexually abused are watching and listening to others all the time, looking for clues as to how the other person feels towards them, or even as to how they should be feeling in a situation themselves. They do this either because they are fearful, or because they are looking to others for love and approval, or both! This behaviour can be irritating to others, and so the person keeps on feeling uncertain and fearful in the face of others' disapproval.

Knowing what you want and what you are feeling, expressing yourself and defining yourself so that others are not having to, and regaining a true self-awareness is the way out of co-dependence. In group or individual therapy there should be a recognition of this need, and constant encouragement to define yourself and not rely on others to define you. Defining yourself should include the recognition of your own warm, loving feelings for others and the ability to express them. It should include being able to ask for warmth and support when you need it. Being either too dependent or too independent leads to isolation.

If the therapist encourages the open expression of all the client's feelings and allows them to be worked through as and when they arise; and if the therapist is willing to work with the conflicts within the therapy relationship, and allows the client to question the work and the therapist's position; then the client can use the therapy relationship to the full, and can be truly reparented.

The explosive, tearful and angry sessions that the client goes through earlier in the therapy as the historical abuse is uncovered and worked through can give way later to working on the more 'everyday' issues in the client's life. The client can then look at their own behaviour in both personal and work relationships and make more real choices in their own life decisions. A therapist should be able to recognize and acknowledge that the real test of progress in therapy is the work that the client does for her or himself out in the world. The client can try out new behaviour, and bring back the outcomes to be discussed and the feelings to be worked on in the next sessions.

Good parenting allows, supports and encourages a child's curiosity, and gives room for questioning and challenging the parents' standards and values. Parents allow their children to develop fully as individuals when they give them the feeling that they have the right to criticize and question their parents' positions and standards on any issue when necessary. Parents and children will ideally feel able to differ from one another, and this lets the children be who they are, a mixture of their own natural character and the experiences and messages they have taken in over the years.

As we have said, when you are in therapy it's important to recognize and feel able to express *all* your feelings, including anger towards your therapist. It's all right to have these feelings, and a therapist should be willing and able to work with them. You may or may not be 'right' to be angry with this person, and you may be transferring something onto them that doesn't belong to them, but you should feel free to 'share' your anger anyway and to check it out. This is something most of us weren't able to do as children, and it is a skill we all need in order to ensure that we stay safe as adults. Perhaps you feel you do have something valid to be angry about. You need to be able to explore it with your therapist and it is your right to be able to do that. In the same way as a good parent would, a therapist must be willing to give up the position of power that they hold, when it's appropriate.

We go to therapy in order to work through the unfinished business that we carry forward into our life from past events, and to look at and work on the behaviour in our lives that is not working for us now. The result of working through early traumas, and expressing the feelings around them that we have previously blocked off and denied, is that we will have access to all our emotions. We should then be free to feel and express them at all the appropriate times in our lives. The goal of therapy is that we should have more choice, and that includes the ability to choose to be angry, sad, or whatever we feel and need to be.

There is another important aspect of the power that a

counsellor or therapist can have in the therapy relationship. The client can give up their own wisdom, knowledge and power to the professional, go to a more childlike place in themselves, and once again deny their own inner wisdom and power. Because many people who have been abused need to regress, to go back to feeling like a child and revisit the feelings they had when they were abused as children, they are vulnerable to being held in this place by their therapist. They do have a legitimate need to go back into the confusion, anger, hurt and pain, and to have their therapist as a witness and comforter in that time. They must be able to visit that childlike place, and then they must be encouraged to return to being as much of an adult as they can be.

A Compassionate and Supportive Response

People who have been abused need to go through the history of their abuse, and have the abuse acknowledged and responded to. Even the simplest kinds of acknowledge-ment of the pain and grief can have very powerful healing effects at these times. Hearing your therapist say 'I'm sorry that happened to you', 'That should not have happened', 'They were wrong to do that to you', 'It wasn't your fault', and other statements of this kind, is very affirming when they are shared sincerely.

At this point, the therapist's ability to feel compassion and to express it can be one of the most powerful experiences in the healing process. When you go for help, you must feel that your therapist or group believes you and understands the effects of childhood sexual abuse. With the belief and understanding of your history should come support in exploring the details of what happened to you as a child. You should feel you have the personal attention of your group or therapist and their compassion for your situation when you were the victim of the abuse.

You should not feel ashamed to talk in therapy about how you are emotionally today, or about what happened to you in the past. There may be things that you are doing now, as a result of your history, that you need to change; but that should be understood, and worked with. Others in a group may feel frustrated and angry with you at times, and that may be appropriate if you are indeed behaving in a frustrating way. You should not, however, feel at the end of the day you are being rejected – it is your behaviour that is being confronted, not all of you. You should feel safe with your group, or your individual therapist, and be able to talk about anything without feeling ashamed. Particularly in a group situation, you should feel safe to use the group as a sounding board. Listen to their feedback about how the group experiences you, and get their help and support in making the changes that you need to make.

When Leila, whom we talked about in chapter two, told her therapist about the men abusing her in the riding stables, her therapist said: 'Didn't you put yourself in some dangerous positions!' There should be no danger in being a 13-year-old girl grooming a horse at nine o'clock on a Saturday morning. When you go for help, steer clear of any therapist or group that seems to disbelieve you or to minimize what happened to you. If you were sexually abused as a child, that will have had a major effect on you. You have a right to work through your history with support, not with disbelief or criticism.

Some professionals are simply still unaware of the significance of a history of childhood sexual abuse, and they will not give the importance to it that your history deserves. Ignorance of the importance of childhood sexual abuse on the part of some professionals can mean long hours of therapy spent 'looking for the issue', when if the history of the abuse was worked with, the issues would quickly become clear.

Some survivors are slow and dreamy, others are speedy and impatient. Like anyone else, survivors deal with their history in their own characteristic way. Therapists are human too, although hopefully they will be more aware of their own particular 'style', and will make an effort to see that their own expectations of you do not get displaced onto you in the form of demands that you should think, feel and perform in ways that the therapist approves of. Your therapist must allow you autonomy and freedom of choice.

WORKING IN GROUPS

For survivors, groups are definitely a good way of working on yourself. Hearing other people's experiences, and comparing them to yours, helps you to uncover parts of your history and put what you already know about yourself in a context. Other people in groups can help us recognize abuse that until then we were unaware of. In a group there will be a good, supportive feeling as you work with others who were abused as children.

You can find groups that are ongoing, which you attend for an indefinite period, and these can be effective therapy and support groups. Most people seem to find groups best if they are led rather than leaderless. It does help if there is someone to have an overview of what is going on in the group, especially to watch out for negative group dynamics, where the group can fragment and begin to concentrate on one or a few group members. The group can then spend a lot of time trying to 'change' them, rather than allowing or demanding that everyone uses the group. There is also, however, great value in leaderless support groups, which are often free of charge, and which give you the opportunity of working on yourself with other survivors for the cost of renting the room they take place in.

Another very useful process is to work in one-off groups. These are short groups that meet over six weeks or so, or for two full days in the week, or over a weekend. They should have a clearly defined aim. You may want to go to a group solely to look at how you deal with your anger or your guilt, or the focus can be historical family therapy, or family sculpting, or reparenting. All of these will give you the opportunity to put together a representation of your own family of origin, and to use other group members to help you play out some of what went on in your family.

You can then go through what happened in your family, either playing it out the way it 'should' have been, or talking about the feelings that come up when you see and feel the situation played out. Or, in working on your anger, you could have another group member play out your father, or mother, or whoever sexually abused you, and explore and express some of the feelings you have for that person or people. You will probably find that other people in the group can relate to your story. They may give you a lot of affirmation and recognition that you were in a bad or abusive situation, and give you support for expressing your feelings about the abuse.

It can be difficult sometimes to hear other people talking about our family of origin. We may feel like defending our family, but, given time, we get used to seeing what went on with less of a sense of defensiveness and actually become more able to see what was really happening for all of the people involved.

Playing out in psychodrama the way it should have been, by constructing your ideal family, can help to put you in touch with the hurt and pain of what your original family felt like to you. This can be difficult at first, but you do see and hear other people in the group get in touch with similar emotions and work through them. You can begin to feel that it's right to get in touch with the feelings and express them, perhaps not in the first group, but maybe in the second. It's right to take it at your own pace, and not to give up.

Going along to one-off groups in this way can really help you to recognize and express some of the feelings you have about your early experiences, and give you much more insight into what was going on in your family. This can add to your individual work with your therapist or counsellor.

In your work in individual and group therapy you can learn to trust your own feelings and make life decisions that include how you feel with others. You can make decisions about your relationships that are based on those feelings. We all need close relationships with people whom we can share our feelings with and who will share how they feel with us.

When you can share your feelings with the people close to you, you can create your own boundaries and go about living your life in the way that is best for you. This can sound selfish, or self-centred, and it is in a way, but in a positive way. We like to share with others, and part of living a life that satisfies us is to make other people feel good too. When we feel safe enough to trust someone and to tell them when we are angry with them, we are less likely to feel that we may destroy the relationship or be destroyed ourselves. We can then be free to be more of ourselves, who we would have been if we had been allowed to express ourselves when we were small.

In this chapter we have looked at going to others for help. In the next, we look at what we can do to help ourselves, whether or not we are in therapy with professionals.

5. What We Can Do Now

In this chapter, we will look at what each of us can do to recover from sexual abuse whether or not we are in therapy. There are many things we can do for ourselves so that we can live our lives to the full and be all we could have been if we had not been abused as children.

For someone who is not in therapy of any sort, change can be difficult. We need the feedback of others in order to make changes. Alone we find it very difficult to see where we're going wrong. We need to hear the opinions of others, and compare their attitudes to what's going on in our lives. With other people's help it will be more possible for us to reflect clearly on who we are, and how we behave. Our own defence against our experience of pain begins when we are very young. We will have honed our defences over the years so that it is difficult to find our way through them and contact our true feelings. If you are willing to go through the exercises that we suggest here and to do them with commitment, they can make a significant difference to how you see yourself and to how you feel about yourself. If you are also willing to share this process with another person that you can trust, then that can have a really useful mutual benefit.

If you are in therapy or in a support group, the exercises that we suggest here can be of great value. Hopefully your therapist or group will be working with your emotional process, and, with the benefit of exercises like these, you can help yourself be much more in touch with your own feelings.

Apart from the deep work that we can do to recover ourselves in therapy, there are ways that we can watch out for ourselves in our everyday lives. As we have seen in other chapters, a legacy of having been sexually abused as a child is that we can easily be abused again. With awareness of others' behaviour, and sensitivity to our own feelings and behaviour, we can negotiate for better relationships, ones that will nurture us. If these relationships cannot be improved, we can learn to let go of them. We can look after ourselves by listening to ourselves and to our true feelings and by having a clearer understanding of what it is that we want and how we want to be.

RECLAIMING OUR FEELINGS

As we begin to look at and work on ourselves, first and foremost we need to recognize that, when children are abused, they learn to block their feelings off in order to lessen the pain and confusion that comes from the abuse. As adults we carry on the same process; the abuse may stop, but the need to defend ourselves from the feelings remains. Usually we are not aware of this blocking process very much, if at all. It is a very efficient process which we began early in childhood and developed for our own personal protection. We do it unconsciously, and it happens as quickly as the blinking of an eye.

The first step in the process of our recovery, therefore, is to reclaim our feelings for ourselves. As we said in the previous chapter, this can be painful at first. We did have a good reason to block our feelings off in the first place.

Getting back in touch with them is not easy or painless. It is necessary, though, if we are to become all that we can be and reclaim all the parts of ourselves.

Our old defences trap us in a world that really belongs to our past. In our lives now we may be behaving inappropriately in all kinds of situations. We may be affecting other people in ways that we would not wish to, and just not know that we are doing it or why people respond to us in the way that they do.

For the practical purpose of beginning the process of reclaiming our feelings, we need to label just what we are looking for. Rex encourages clients to begin the process of looking at their feelings by looking out for the six basic emotions:

Fear

What we mean by this is not just the abject fear that we can all have when something terrible happens to us, but all the other smaller fearful responses too. If we are more aware of these, our responses to the situations that we meet in our everyday lives can be surer, and we can be more true to ourselves. So we would include here: anxiety, feeling scared or trembly, the feeling of dread, fright, stage fright, performance anxiety, alarm, panic, hopelessness, nervousness, lack of confidence, hesitation, avoidance, apprehension, nerves, having 'butterflies' or jitters.

Love

Once again, we are not just looking at the passion of romantic love; there are lots of different kinds of love. If we begin to recognize that we are feeling loving in a situation where before we were unaware of it, this too can inform how we behave with these people in these situations. We would include here: warmth, care, friendliness, liking, appreciation, kindness, tenderness, fondness, devotion, loyalty, admiration.

Anger

Anger is a difficult, painful and frightening feeling for many people, and is ignored completely by others. Anger is seen as a negative emotion, and, if it is not properly handled, it can be. Too many people 'dump' their anger inappropriately on others, putting it where it does not belong. Probably all of us have experienced an angry confrontation or put-down from someone which does not really belong to us but to some other relationship or situation. Even if someone is angry with us, we need not let them put us down or attack us.

People can have a real fear of either their own anger or other people's getting 'out of control', and not want to recognize or express their anger at all. But the reality is that anger is a powerfully positive emotion too and, handled properly, its main use is as our boundary maker. Anger can be seen as the person's feelings saying, 'I don't like this, I don't want it to happen, I would like to do something about it.' Or it can give us information such as, 'I don't feel comfortable with this; I would like something different to happen here.' Recognizing these feelings can lead to our leaving a situation; anger can provide the 'escape velocity' that gets us out. It may not always be the best way to get out, but it is better than staying and being abused, or carrying on doing something that you feel bad or uncomfortable about.

When you look out for your angry feelings, notice irritability, resentment, discontent, surliness, impatience, taking offence, bitterness, hard feelings, hate, holding grudges, being fierce, 'having a bone to pick', frustration, crabbiness, and feeling furious, fed-up, vindictive, vengeful, spiteful, malicious, irate, shirty, exasperated and bad tempered.

Grief

Grief is best thought of as a mixture of anger and sadness. It's important to remember the anger, as most often grieving tends to be looked at as sadness.

However, there will almost always be anger around too – even, for instance, in the case of someone dying, where there can be the angry feeling that goes with being left. Grief does not end until you are really finished with working it through. In our society we sometimes seem to believe that people should get over a death or loss quite quickly, and be able to get on with their lives in the usual way. In fact grieving takes much longer if the feelings are denied and not talked through and expressed. There should not be any rush.

Sadness

Here we need to be careful, because sadness is seen as an acceptable emotion in pretty much the same way that anger is seen as an unacceptable one. So if you find it is much easier to make a long list of what you are feeling sad about than what you are feeling angry about, then it's worth experimenting with substituting anger for sadness on the same list. It may give you some idea of the anger that you are hiding from yourself. A lot of people avoid looking at their anger by focusing on their sadness instead.

We would include under the heading of sadness: feeling 'blue', suffering, heartache, angst, sorrow, despondency, regret, worry, unease, fretting, cares, troubles, unhappiness, dreariness, disillusionment, disappointment, despair, hopelessness, and feeling down, depressed, teary, upset, fed-up.

Joy

Strangely enough, for such a positive emotion, joy tends to go unrecognized and unexpressed. When we ignore our pleasure over the small things in life, and stay with the big worries, our life becomes distorted and we lose perspective.

Include in your list when you look for joy: pleasure, fun, enjoyment, being thrilled, delighted, happy, feelings of well-being, ease, satisfaction, amusement, feeling pleased, glad, good, smiley, excited, terrific, that 'punching the air' feeling, plus any more you can think of!

We've put the basic feelings in that order simply because they spell FLAGS Joy, which helps us to remember what the basic ones are. They are not in any order of importance. Far from it – we attach the same importance to them all. We know that they all have the power to help us to change our lives when we recognize them and take them into account. They all affect us deeply in our dealings with the world.

We find it useful to think of the feelings as shown up on a bar chart, or like the flickering lights on a hi-fi system which show the differing levels of pitch as the music is played. Sometimes one tone will be muted, with hardly anything showing at all, while at other times it seems that all the tones are going at full pitch.

If you find that concept useful, try to imagine a couple of examples. Say you wake up in the morning, and you realize today is the day you have a job interview or assessment that matters a lot to you. You could possibly guess that your levels of feeling would look like this:

FEAR	LOVE	ANGER	GRIEF	SADNESS	JOY

And then imagine that you have a very successful interview, you are offered the job, and the salary is a little more than you thought it would be. Your feeling chart could look like this:

FEAR	LOVE	ANGER	GRIEF	SADNESS	JOY

107

This is a simple and obvious example. It may not always be that easy to keep track of just what is going on at a feeling level, but with practice, especially if you do it consistently, you will learn to recognize how you are being affected by what is going on around you in the here and now.

There may also be feelings from old issues coming up, and it's useful to be aware of those too. For example, when you get the new job, you may be sad that a person that you love is not present to share your happiness with you. If it's someone who has died, there may be grief about them not seeing you get the job, or perhaps anger at the way they always undermined you by telling you that you were no good.

We have given just a few ideas and examples of feelings that might crop up in particular situations. We are all so richly different that it's impossible to guess what your individual feelings will be. Try to be open to all of them, and allow yourself to be surprised sometimes by the result. Be an explorer of your own inner feelings.

We believe that it is important to stay quite strictly with the six basic emotions at the beginning in order to avoid getting into 'blind alleys' around emotions like 'upset' or 'hurt'. We have left out 'hurt', for example, because it tends to be unspecific; the underlying emotion is probably anger, as the implication is that someone must have attacked us in order for us to be 'hurt'. Similarly, if we are feeling 'vulnerable', the implication is that someone is ready to bully or attack us. In both of these examples we would be focusing on other people's behaviour towards us, and not staying with our own feelings. What we are actually feeling inside can easily remain unclear unless we concentrate on our own feelings. It is better for us to own that we are angry, or fearful, or whatever our feelings are, and then take action for ourselves, than it is for us to begin from a 'you hurt me and I am a victim' position. We are more self-reliant and able to make positive choices when we can recognize what we feel first. We can then confront the people that we need to at the time that we choose, in what seems the best way for us.

We can add jealousy and envy to the list and be aware of those feelings too. We are thinking here of jealousy in the sense that you would guard something or someone jealously, and fear losing them, and envy in the sense that you envy someone who is having a relationship with a person that you would like to be with, or who has something that you want. When you envy someone, you want to take what they have from them, whether it is a possession or a person, or you want to destroy the object or the person so that they cannot have them.

The important thing to remember, as you try to track your emotions, is that *all* your feelings are there, *all* the time. You will need to be careful that you do not track only what we call your 'preferred' emotions. These are not the emotions that you choose to feel because you like them, but the familiar ones that you have identified with over the years and that have become the ones that you recognize yourself by.

Self-Assessment

Take a moment now to think of how you would describe yourself. Would you think of yourself as 'a nice person', perhaps jovial, with a good sense of humour? Would you think of yourself as strictly adult, standing no nonsense, 'not suffering fools gladly'? Spend some time now looking at all the major aspects of your 'self'. How would you generally recognize yourself? Perhaps as a good daughter or son, or a bad one; a good worker, or a bad one; a good mother or father, or a bad one.

You may find your view of yourself changes from day to day. You may need to make several lists, perhaps one for each day for a week, and take time to get an overall view. You may see your 'self' differently from day to day, but you should find certain aspects of 'you' that you can recognize consistently.

Include in your lists how you see yourself physically. Do you see yourself as attractive or unattractive? Also include whether you see yourself as safe and secure or unsafe, friendly or nasty, trustworthy or not, and any other things that you can think of to define who you are.

Now take a few moments to think about how you imagine that other people would describe you. Make a list of your friends, colleagues, acquaintances and family, and list the words or phrases they would use about you. We want to emphasize at this point that this is *your* interpretation, that we are looking at how *you* think others see and experience you. See if you can get a clear idea of who you are to yourself and to the people close to you. When you have completed this self-assessment, then you may want to try checking these feelings out with your family, friends or colleagues.

When you have kept a note over several days or a week, look to see what the predominant emotions are. If you have a complete set of FLAGS Joy there, see which ones occur most often. Do they fit in with events in your life? Are they 'appropriate' to what is going on?

See too if there are any feelings that are missing altogether, or figure very little, and think about why they are not there as a regular part of your life. Are you avoiding feelings that you find uncomfortable? Try to be really honest with yourself. Looking at missing feelings and seeing how you avoid them or change them is a first step in working on yourself. For example, you may not acknowledge your anger but change it into sadness.

WORKING THROUGH ANGER

Most people are afraid of their anger. Anger is not a popular emotion in our society, and we are mostly encouraged to suppress it, particularly when we are growing up. Usually, people would much prefer that we are quiet and adapt to them, rather than have to deal with our expression of angry feelings and our being able to take a position for ourselves.

Anger is a powerful emotion, and can be uncomfortable to get in touch with, but you do have a right to be angry about what happened to you. You need to recognize the anger that you buried long ago and express it in order to work your way through it. Every person that has been violated and sexually abused has the right to be angry about what happened to them. Your irreplaceable childhood was stolen, and you are left to pick up the pieces on your own.

You may want to excuse what happened to you, to say it was partly your fault, or *all* your fault. Remember, it is *never* the child's fault. The adult or caretakers always have the responsibility. It is true that in some situations our caretakers may have been so damaged themselves that they were unable to care properly for us. This does not mean that we have to make excuses for them and undermine our right to be angry. Our priority must be to deal with how we feel about what happened to us. Every child has a right to a happy and safe childhood. It was not your fault that you were abused.

Don't forget too that part of being taken care of as a child is knowing that your caretaker is watching out for you, and this includes being aware of changes in your behaviour if something bad is happening to you. Every child has a right to that kind of protection. If you were not protected, you have a right to be angry about that.

If you are working through your feelings about being abused as a child, it is important to overcome your resistance to expressing the sound of your anger. Anyone working on their anger needs to make noise, as it is only then that you can hear your own anger. You need to be loud enough to feel that you are putting out more anger than you have before, so that you begin to expand the boundaries of your anger.

Beginning to deal with your anger can be a frightening thing to do, especially if you are alone. What we are suggesting here is that you do it at your own pace; it is very important not to push yourself too far too quickly. If you begin to feel a fear that you cannot overcome on your own, then it is important that you find someone that you can trust to be with you as you work with your anger and give you the support that you need.

Anger Exercises

If you are in a situation where no one else can hear you, and you can make as much noise as you need to, then use the exercises described on the following pages to do just that. If you are in a small flat with neighbours who will overhear, do the quieter exercises we suggest here, but put out as much sound as you feel able to, and the more the better.

We use plastic baseball bats or tennis rackets to beat cushions, and we make sounds, preferably angry words. Use angry language, try swearing, experiment with being angry – see if you can find other ways of expressing yourself than your habitual ones. The language of our anger needn't be inhibited when we are expressing it to a pillow or a towel. When people are angry you see them stamp, bang things with their hands, make angry sounds, and use angry language. You can do the same natural things, and remember that you have a right to be angry about what happened to you.

We recommend that you set time aside regularly, ideally daily, to work out your anger. This is a vital part of working through the feelings that you have about what happened to you as a child.

Make a space for yourself where you will not be disturbed, and where you can have a large cushion opposite you. You can imagine the person you are angry with is standing or sitting there, or you can simply use the cushion as a focus for your anger.

Sit quietly for a few minutes, with your thoughts of what happened to you, or your memories. If you cannot exactly remember what happened to you, that doesn't matter. Your work with your anger will liberate memories over a period of time.

Now allow yourself to really feel your anger. If you have a bat or a racket, you may want to hit the cushion. If you fear making a noise because of people overhearing you, take a towel and wring it between your hands. Begin to hit the pillow or wring the towel. Let yourself feel your anger, and begin to growl or scream. It's really important that you let yourself make a sound, because you will begin to feel more as you hear yourself being angry.

As you express your anger, you may lose some control and get very angry – that is fine. You will need to tell your angry story regularly until you are finished and done with being angry. Then after a while the angry feelings will come back again, and you will want to use your anger rituals again. Working through your anger can be done regularly, and being in touch with it and expressing it regularly is a healthy thing to do.

If you're working with a towel, try biting it and growling as loud as you can. Or try hitting the part of your abuser that offended you – if it was their penis, their mouth, or whatever, visualize that part on the pillow and *hit them there!*

You may want to tear up old telephone directories, or get in touch with your angry feelings while you're doing chores. Some people use their anger while they're chopping wood for the stove.

Don't be frightened to scream or growl and make a noise, especially if you can find a friend who is willing to help you in this way, to be there with you while you cry and rage. You may feel really angry, or perhaps a mixture of anger and despair. These are natural, although it can sound very frightening when you or someone you know gets in touch with this depth of feeling. Try not to let the depth or noise of your emotions stop you from expressing your feeling. Just imagine how it feels to be small and to have someone, whom you deeply need to love you, sexually abuse you for their own reassurance or pleasure. Or maybe someone you didn't know at all, a complete stranger, just came along and took advantage of your vulnerability and did this to you. As a child you would have felt and suppressed huge

114

conflicts and depths of emotion, and it's time to begin to let it out. It's OK to do it now. You are safe, and working the abusive situation out in this way will make you safer.

Above all, take care of yourself while you are working with the bat, or with any of these exercises. Watch out for your back – if you have a weak back or a problem back, look for other exercises. Don't abuse yourself, and be aware of your needs. It's important to take the time that you need to work through these feelings, so don't rush it.

If you can find someone you trust, get support for yourself. It's very good to have people give you affirmations when you are beating up pillows. They will be able to encourage you to get into your anger, and when they feel you are really getting angry they can shout along with you, 'Yes, yes, that's it! Do it! Do it!'

If you are working with or supporting someone in working on their anger in this way, you must be aware of the fine line between helping and encouraging someone, and abusing or frightening them. Remember that the easiest people to abuse are those who have a history of being abused, and that people have to be ready to work on these issues. Let them work in their own time and at their own pace.

Recognizing Our Own Abusive Parts

Once we have looked at our own anger, we can begin to look at the abusive parts of ourselves. It is very easy to lose touch with the fact that we take in what happens to us on a deep level, and that includes the abuser's behaviour. Somewhere inside of us there is often hidden away the memory of the way our abuser was, and there is a real need to get to know our own abusive parts so that we're in charge of them rather than them being in charge of us. For all of us who have been abused it can be chilling to recognize that we have an abusive part too.

Once we recognize that abusive part and get to know it, we can do two things. First, we can own it. We can accept that *we* really have this part in us, and that in some situations we almost certainly bring it out – not in sexually abusing children, but in abusing others in some way. Perhaps we do this by not respecting their feelings or their needs, or perhaps by being impatient with children or strangers. We have seen this in ourselves, and in many other people whom we have worked with. We can take in the abuse and pass it on, just as adults who were physically abused as children may feel the impulse to hit out at their own children.

Second, we can get angry at the person who abused us and 'taught' us this way of behaving to others.

A way of discovering and working with the abusive part of us is to play out our abuser. Try sitting on the other pillow and talking back to yourself, using the language of your abuser(s). Act them out one at a time if there were more than one. Behave as the abuser did when he or she was abusing you.

One important thing to recognize is that we may be using the same abusive behaviour that we learnt in our childhood to carry on abusing ourselves now. See what happens when you play out the part of you that abuses you now, your own vicious critic that says you are no good. That internal critic may well be abusing other people too. Play out that part, and see how you frighten yourself with the nastiness of your internal critic.

Although it can be scary to look at the part of us that has

taken on the abusive behaviour when we're trying to heal the abuse we've received, we do have a responsibility to ourselves to explore our own abusive part as well as looking at how we were victims of others' abusive behaviour.

We may feel vengeful too, and it can be good to act out the revenge. As you are using the bat, or whatever anger exercise you do, think of what you would like to do to the person who abused you, or what you would have liked to have happened to them. Don't worry if the fantasies are outrageous. If you have these fantasies, play them out, let yourself work them through in your work with the cushions.

Another way that we can use two cushions is to put the abuser on the cushion and talk to them as our strong adult selves now, thereby imagining that it is we who have the power now. We need to tell our abuser as loudly as we can what we think of an adult or parent that would sexually abuse a little child. Explore your feelings and let yourself have your anger as a powerful woman or man in the world. Tell them, if you think they were unwell, that they should have got help for themselves and not acted out with you sexually. Or that they should have been picked up by the police, or recognized as abusers by others and had something done about them, and that, anyway, they should have been stopped from abusing you.

If you have ambivalent feelings about your abuser, for example if they were a loving and caring person who was good to you most of the time, someone who you would still want to have a good relationship with, you may want to put two cushions out in front of you. You can then separate out the part of them that is totally unacceptable to you, the part that abused you, and freely express your angry reactions to that part. When you feel warm or caring feelings come

117

up in you, express them strictly to the other, 'good person' pillow. Then you can explore the good/bad father, or mother or other caretaker, and get clear of the confusion between the good and bad parts of them that this kind of ambivalence brings.

As you work on your anger and become clear about it, you will be different in the way you are with the rest of the world. You will be more assertive, and people will experience you differently. This may be the time that you become aware of other people's resistance to the changes in you. If you are still in touch with your family, they will find you different too by degrees. You may experience their resistance. Your anger and your ability to take more of a position for yourself may stir up their unresolved feelings. They will probably have a strong investment in you staying the way you've always been.

CONFRONTING YOUR ABUSER

The other issue that may come up for you as you feel stronger in yourself is whether you want to confront directly the person or people that abused you. You may also want to confront someone that you feel should have helped or protected you, but who let you down at the time.

If you decide to confront them, you probably should take someone with you who understands you and your situation. We recommend that you take someone who would be willing to take your part if the abuser denies what happened to you and starts to put you down and attack you. In our experience, this very often happens. People tend to be consistent, and an abuser who denied your reality years ago may very well do exactly the same thing to you now. This can be very undermining, and it's the best reason to take someone along with you for support.

There is also the issue of your relationship with the abuser now. If you were abused years ago, that person may have changed a good deal: they may have mellowed, or they may be old and frail now. Maybe your relationship with them has changed too. Perhaps the truest place to confront the person who actually abused you is in your room with your cushions.

To confront your abuser and have them acknowledge that they did what they did, and apologize to you for it, must be one of the best and most relieving things that can happen to us. Unfortunately, it does seem to be rare for this to happen; most abusers become very defensive, and sometimes very aggressive. So our advice is not to go alone. If you then want to confront the person on your own, you can take them aside in another room and speak to them personally. You will still have your supporter right there for you when you come out from speaking to them.

FORGIVENESS

When we are abused as children, we do have a huge problem to deal with. Our feelings of anger, invasion and pain are enormous. What many of us did to cope with these feelings was to abuse other children, or animals. Many survivors feel terribly bad about having been cruel to family pets or wild creatures, brothers and sisters, or to other children, or for doing sexual things that we now regret. It is worth remembering the kind of pressure that we were under at the time, not to excuse ourselves, but to put our behaviour in a context. To help resolve what happened, you might try putting the animal, sibling(s) or other children on one of your cushions and have a dialogue with them about what happened and about how you were. You may want to apologize for what you did. You may also want to be forgiven for it.

Forgiveness from others may be a big thing for us if we have abused, and this raises the issue of whether we can ever forgive our abusers too. Some survivors of childhood sexual abuse find the whole issue of whether to forgive very difficult. They feel they should 'forgive and forget', but at the same time they know they still feel very angry.

Rex once went to give a presentation at a Rabbinical College in London. There was a man in the audience whose whole family had been destroyed in the Holocaust. He believed that nothing was worked through until you could forgive the perpetrators of what had happened to you. He had worked hard to forgive the people who had killed his whole family.

We believe that it is possible to forgive. But whether it is possible to forgive people who are close to you, or even strangers, whose personal choice it is to sexually abuse a child, *has* to be left to the person who has been abused. You are the person who is left with the feelings. They can walk away, but you can't.

Someone else at the Rabbinical College said, 'We forgive, but we never forget.' This idea of letting go, but remaining vigilant against the possibility of further abuse, seems sensible to us.

We also know many people who neither forgive nor forget, and we fully support this. Part of making a recovery from abuse is to be angry about it. If in the fullness of time forgiveness feels appropriate, it will be, and that is fine. You may never want to forgive, or never feel like forgiving, and that is fine too.

RECLAIMING YOUR MEMORIES

A possibly less stressful way of reclaiming your childhood memories and working through the feelings you have about what happened to you is to make a life line. Take a long sheet of paper – lining paper, wrapping paper or computer printing paper – and draw a line down it lengthways. Let this line represent the length of your life up to now. You can do a longer line that leads into the future if you want to.

Now write down the dates of your life. Start with the year of your birth, then add the subsequent years with your age beside them. Write down the good and the bad things that happened to you beside the years when they were happening. You may want to do this simply in a straight date order, or you may want to identify significant events that you remember and put the dates in later. You can write in pencil at first if you are like most survivors of abuse and have only a hazy memory of your past.

The idea of this exercise is to enable you to get much clearer about your history. This will give you a context to put in other memories as you recover them. Again, this could take a while. You should see it as a process that you will leave from time to time, and then come back to, as and when other memories slot into their place. You may realize, for example, that something couldn't have happened on a certain day, but must have taken place after your sister was born, or whatever other milestones you can come up with as you reclaim your past. Treat it as an exploration, and don't be hard on yourself if you can't remember. Memories will come back to you.

If you know people who knew you at the time and you feel safe to go to them, speak with them about what they saw happening. You may get other ideas to fill in any blank areas that you have in your life line. You may want to do your life line several times; you don't have to get it right all at once.

You can also take whatever photographs you have of yourself from that time and sit down with them. Think about what was happening in your life, and see how you looked then. Take your time – try to set aside a little time every day to sit with yourself, and with a friend if you have one you can take into your confidence. Write a little every day or when you can.

Now take a look at what happened to you as you've written it down. How would you feel if you heard that a little person in that situation had been treated that way? Give yourself time to look over your writings, the photographs, and the life line. Let yourself experience the range of feelings that you have as you look at your own story set out there, and give yourself the time you need to express those feelings. Use any of the exercises we have suggested already, for example the cushion work with the bat, or sitting the abuser on the other cushion, or you could try speaking to your child inside you now about the hurt that she or he experienced then.

You can go back to the life line exercise whenever you want to, and you will probably recover more of your history every time. Use it as one of the tools to reclaim your history and your memories for your self.

CARING FOR THE INNER CHILD

Another very important way for us to move on from the legacy of having been sexually abused as a child is to work with the child who was abused and who we still carry within us.

Early memories of what happened to us, whether it was good or bad, live on inside us. We have looked at how to recall those memories. The memory of how *we* were – how we felt, how we thought and probably how we spoke – is there too. Most of us keep a childlike place inside us for ever.

The only person who can take care of that child inside now is us. No one else can see what she or he needs, so no one else can fulfil those needs. You can take care of the small child inside you with the adult person that you have become.

It's important to have that balance between our adult and child parts, because being an adult who still feels like a hurt and lonely child can be a real handicap. Other adults may feel that you have no right to be a child; why should you be childlike when they are strong and adult? You, on the other hand, still feel childlike, maybe small, maybe hurt and angry. Since you have not been properly parented, you may feel it should be your turn to be a child and be taken care of now! It is very unlikely that this will happen. It seems to us that the most you can hope for is caring people around you who are willing to accept your vulnerability and who will respond to you when you ask for what you really need, when it's appropriate.

The fact is that adults who behave like needy children are generally unattractive to the rest of the world. Adult survivors of childhood sexual abuse often have child parts that feel they deserve the love they never got from the adults around them when they were small. In reality, we have to grow up for ourselves, without having had a proper childhood in the first place. If this seems unfair to you, it is – this is the legacy of having been sexually abused. That may well make you very angry, and we think that's an appropriate feeling.

If we do not listen to the needs of our own inner child, the likelihood is that no one else will. If our inner child is not listened and responded to, she or he will become more desperate, and have more effect on our way of being in the world. We will be less adult, and more childlike. If we do not take responsibility for ourselves, we are likely to go on expecting others to be responsible for us, and this is disastrous for relationships.

When we learn to cherish our child part, and to look after our inner needs, we can be more outgoing in the world and more present with other people. When our inner child recognizes that our adult part will not be neglectful, abusive and denying, she or he can relax and enjoy life, and give up the demanding neediness and attention seeking.

So have a dialogue with your inner child. Put her or him on the pillow opposite you and hear what she or he has to say. Listen closely. Let your own child inside you tell you what she or he needs: for example, to feel safe and more secure, to eat, or to sleep more. Let your list be as long as the needs are. The list may be very long the first time around; this little child has not been asked what she or he wants for a long time!

Make a note of each thing, and try not to worry about whether it is possible to fulfil these needs. Hear them first, and together you and your inner child will find a way to do them later. You will find a way that just feels right, and you will know that your inner child's needs are being met. You will both feel satisfied.

We think of intuition as 'inner tuition'; let your inner child be the voice that teaches you. Ask questions about who the people are that you want to spend most time with, and how much time you take off from your work to rest or to play. People who have contact and dialogue with their inner child are likely to feel better about themselves. Our inner child can tell us how to nourish ourselves well, if we listen.

SELF-NURTURING

In order to take care of yourself, it's best to spend time only with people who make you feel good about yourself. Learn to trust your feelings on this too. Work only with people you trust. You may need to negotiate for what you really want in a relationship. If you really cannot get what you want in that relationship, then you may have to leave it. We believe that it is better to get up and walk away from a situation where you are abused, even if you are alone and have to start out all over again, than it is to stay.

As we learn to listen to ourselves and validate our needs, we develop a sense of entitlement. We begin to recognize that we deserve good things and good relationships, and that we need to take time to take care of ourselves.

See if you can discover ways to nurture yourself, to give yourself something for once. We can develop the feeling that we deserve good things, like warm rooms, good clothes, nice baths with bath oils, and any of the things that we really like and feel nourished by.

We can learn to give ourselves positive affirmations, to say to ourselves, 'Whatever it takes I'm going to do it', or,

'I survived, and I deserve to feel good about myself.' See if there are affirmations that ring true for you that can be your special affirmations.

RECLAIMING THE BODY

You will notice that the examples of nurturing we gave covered bathing, warmth and good clothes – self-nourishing things that are focused on the body. We find that looking after the body does not come high on the list of priorities of many of the survivors that we have worked with. This can be because of generally low self-esteem and poor self-image, or it can be specifically because our abused body seems vulnerable, or bad. We may even feel that our body let us down by being abused in the first place – some people remember their body responding with pleasurable feelings to the sexual abuse.

Our body is a part of who we are. Some people believe that all we are is our body and that all our thoughts, feelings and processes go on there; they feel that they don't exist anywhere else. So rejecting our body, or refusing to be kind and gentle to it, or even harming and punishing it, is dangerously close to being at war with ourselves. Forgiving your body for responding to any pleasure it may have felt during the abuse is vital to becoming whole again. Just as it was not your fault that you were abused, it wasn't your body's fault either. Your body was probably the focus of the assault on who you are and who you were. Your body now deserves to be forgiven and cared for. We think the anger that you may feel and show to your body really belongs to the person or people who abused you.

Just as you as a child could not give consent, so your body

was not able to give consent. As well as the emotional responses to being sexually abused, a child also has to deal with the confusion at her or his own body's responses to the abuse. The fact is that our bodies do sometimes respond to stimulation, of any kind. If when you were abused your body had a sexual or pleasurable response, your body was simply responding to being stimulated. Your body was not having a chosen and pleasurable response, and was not willingly participating.

If we don't recognize that it was not our body's fault, or our fault, we will probably carry on feeling guilty, and have difficulty in listening to our bodily needs as an adult.

A good way of beginning the process of reclaiming our body from the memories of the abuse, and back into a relationship with us, is to build up a feeling connection. We can first of all do a simple thing, which is to bathe consciously, using our favourite oils and taking our time, and then to spend time simply looking at our body in a mirror, or to use several mirrors to get an all-round look at ourselves. After bathing, we can dry ourselves gently and carefully, and give our body some of the healing and caring touch that it needs.

Again, this is a process that you need to take your time over. Your attitude to your body may not change overnight, and we need to be consistent in paying good attention to our bodies so that we can heal our body memories.

As it is so much to do with the senses, working on recovering your body can include drawing. You can take paper and use different coloured crayons to draw how you see yourself in the mirrors, or how you see yourself in your mind's eye. Draw your face, and all the rest of your body, and see if there are any parts that you have a resistance to drawing. If you feel you would like to reclaim these parts, draw them. Do them from a distance first, then let yourself see more detail and draw more detail when you can. Slowly find your way back to a relationship with your body and with the parts that you feel less comfortable with.

Touch

Touch is an issue that can have a great deal of charge around it for survivors of sexual abuse. Some survivors crave touch, really feeling a great need for the comfort that can come from being touched. For other survivors, touch is an absolute taboo. Their boundaries have been crossed too many times in too terrible a way for touch to feel at all safe.

If you do therapy or self-help groups, people in the groups may want to hug you because they feel warm and friendly towards you as you work through and share your experiences. If you have a problem with hugs and touch, let people know about it; you can then ask for hugs if and when you want them. Regulating how and when people touch you, and feeling in control of what happens to your body in this way, is vital if you are to feel safe. In all the exercises that we have talked about we have emphasized the need to pace yourself, and this is no exception. It's all part of getting over the effects of the abuse.

We can experiment with how close we sit to someone by moving away and coming back, playing the accordion of contact. We can do the same thing with time, for instance making a conscious choice about how long we touch for, or choosing carefully how long we meet with someone for. We must ensure that we take all the time we need to keep up to our boundaries, practising 'this far and no further' for ourselves.

KEEPING A JOURNAL

Keeping a journal of your thoughts and feelings can be the most important tool for keeping in touch with your 'self'. This will provide you with the greatest affirmation of your richness and variety.

Your notes and drawings, your dreams and your memories of your changing moods all give you an overview that will keep you going through the bad times when you think you are not worth bothering about. Keeping the journal will help you to get a sense of all of who you are, so you don't lose that sense in the bad times. Use really nice books that you will want to keep, or loose-leaf files that you can put anything you want into. You can keep it like a scrapbook of your work on your self.

This should be your book, or books, that you keep for yourself, where you write up your own process. You can keep it private, or share it, but *only if you want to*. It must be your own decision – you deserve privacy for your most intimate thoughts and recollections. You may write it for a day and then not look at it for months. That's OK too, just don't throw it out! One day you will want to look at it again.

It's well worth keeping a note of your dreams and seeing the patterns that emerge over a period of time. Dreams and even nightmares are a vital part of beginning to pay attention to ourselves, part of our process of uncovering who we are. They often show us parts of ourselves or issues that we do not want to own or deal with.

Keep a special file or folder for things that make you happy, maybe images that cheer you up, or letters of love, support or praise. Make a note whenever anyone says something affirming to you, and use those notes as a resource for yourself when you feel down.

Writing out what happened to you and recording your feelings can take a long time, so give yourself the time it takes to let the painful things that you would rather forget come to the surface and be worked through. When you are working on processing your feelings, whether you are doing letters, your journal, some artwork, or whatever, if you feel you can't do any more, don't. STOP. Withdraw, rest, get support, and stroke yourself for the work that you have done so far.

We would like to conclude this chapter by emphasizing a couple of important points. First, give yourself plenty of time. Don't rush or put pressure on yourself when you are working through the exercises. Do only what you can, and what you want to, and then move on, when you are ready, to whatever you want to do next. Be sure that you make time to appreciate yourself for all the work you're doing.

Second, you don't have to be on your own now. There is a real benefit in having someone else to support you and to feed back to you, so that you get insight into your own behaviour. With insight and reflection we may decide that we want to change our behaviour, or we may keep it the same, but it will be a conscious and aware choice, not an unconscious reaction to a situation. That way of choosing how we are is the way to freedom.

So don't do this work on your own unless you really cannot find anyone you trust enough to share it with. In that case it's a good idea to work on your own until you do find someone else to work with you. That may be another survivor, or it may be a support group. These groups are blossoming, and it may be that you can get in touch with other survivors in your neighbourhood when you feel able to, and work with them. If you don't see any groups advertised, look out for the number of your local Rape Crisis Line, as they often help people who are survivors of childhood sexual abuse too.

In the next chapter we look at how some of the people whom we have talked about in this book have made changes in their lives.

6. There is Always Time

It's never too late to begin the healing process. There is always time to work these issues out for yourself. The abuse may have happened to you a long while ago, and perhaps over a long period of time. There's no need to rush now. In fact it's important to take as much time as you really need. Giving yourself the luxury of really taking this time to work through what happened to you is a vital part of caring for yourself. It takes an enormous amount of time to understand and process the feelings that come up, and to integrate inner changes into the day-to-day activities and interactions in your life. It's also important to appreciate yourself for your courage in facing your abusive past at every stage of the process, and for the fact that you survived the abuse as well as you did.

So many people have forgotten their abuse, and regain the memories of it only gradually. Perhaps there is a good reason for that. It may be that we are only able to remember our abuse when we have the inner resources to begin to cope with the memories.

If you're with a partner, they may want to be involved in the process. It can be an opportunity for you both to learn the value of caring for yourselves. Many people who have been abused unknowingly choose partners who have also been abused. Very often when one person in a couple begins to have memories, this triggers off memories in their partner.

The process of recovery and working in a therapeutic

context is certainly not confined to young people. Memories of abuse can come to people at any time in their lives.

It's important to make a positive commitment to working on these issues; it doesn't just happen. With support and help over varying lengths of time, all the people we talked to and have discussed in this book have been making positive changes in their lives.

Margaret, whom we talked about in chapter three, is now in her late forties. She talks about the time it has taken her to get back in touch with her memories, and says that the process is still going on. She decided that she was going to do whatever it took to heal herself. She has begun the process of valuing herself, and in making this commitment to herself her feelings of self-worth have increased.

Recovering hidden memories and triggering flashes of insight or images of things that happened many years ago has an enormous effect on us, which may be painful and difficult at times. However, as we said in chapter five, we do need to go through this process in order to acknowledge our past and leave it behind us so that we can live fully in the present.

Margaret feels that getting these memories back continues to be useful, and that talking about the memories rather than repressing them means that she is more in control of her life. She doesn't feel that this happens at the expense of her current life, and she and her partner are very present for each other. Talking about the abuse and sharing the grief and pain has brought them very close together.

The abuse is something that happened, however many years ago it may be. Nothing can change that. If the memories are coming back then it's important to look after yourself as well as possible. This can include talking to someone about them and getting support for yourself.

In her professional life, Margaret is allowing herself the luxury of doing the kind of work she wants to and has organized it so that she can work from home. She is happy to earn less money in order to treat herself in a kind and nurturing way.

She has a partner who is willing to share her work on her abuse with her and is able to support her in doing this at workshops and at home. They often spend time reparenting each other, taking it in turns to provide nurturing support for each other's inner child, and doing things like giving each other gentle loving baths and massages. They have also done workshops on intimate communication skills together, which has helped them to talk through the painful issues that have come up. They are aware when feelings come up that have more to do with their past than with their current reality. They are careful to help one another to work through these historical feelings and issues so that they do not have a negative effect on the relationship.

Recently Margaret's partner decorated the bathroom and she found herself feeling ill every time she went into the newly decorated room. She then remembered that the bathroom her family had when she was a child was the same colour, and she knew that that was where her father had abused her. There is another room in Margaret's house which is also that colour and it doesn't affect her. Her partner repainted the bathroom when she told him about it and Margaret immediately felt better. She felt loved, respected and supported by her partner.

Encouraging and supporting a partner in working

through their history, and moving on, is so much better than sticking to the position that 'you should be over it by now'. This position usually comes from the fear that if you indulge someone who has been abused they will never stop wanting to be indulged and will carry on wanting special attention for ever. Many of us have been brought up to be unable to express our needs and feelings or to ask directly for what we want and need. Giving people what they want is not a bad thing.

Margaret worked as a psychotherapist and built up a thriving practice. As very traumatic memories have continued to come back to her, however, she has now freed herself from a feeling that she ought to be helping others, and has allowed herself time in her life to care for herself.

This feeling that we should spend our time caring for others rather than for ourselves is a common one amongst children from dysfunctional families. Family members are often brought up to think of others primarily and not to be so 'selfish' as to put their own needs first. Many of us have been brought up not to recognize our own needs or to feel good about ourselves or our own efforts in life. Too much praise was thought to encourage us to be 'big-headed' and 'full of ourselves'. It can take a lot of personal work to recognize that taking care of ourselves and recognizing our needs is not bad for us, but can actually help us to be fuller and more generous people in the world.

Gail is now able to talk openly about the abuse she suffered and the difficulties it has left her with. She has much more self-esteem and is allowing herself time to do things that she feels good about. She is going to group therapy, although so far she has only felt safe enough to be open and trusting in women's groups. She is also finally allowing herself time off work so that she can be with herself and discover the things that she really wants to do.

Using the support she got from working in therapy, Gail wrote to her parents about the abuse in the family. Shortly after she wrote, and while her mother was away, her father rang her. Gail was alone at home at the time. All the old feelings of being under his control came back when she heard him on the telephone, and she put the phone down. Her father wrote to her saying that he couldn't remember any of what she had written about in her letter, and would she please leave them alone as they were both now old and frail. The reality is that Gail's parents are both healthy and very fit. Her father specifically asked Gail not to contact her mother, despite her having said in her letter to him that she hoped he would not stand in the way of her seeing her mother. Gail felt that he had put pressure on her mother so that they would present a united front in the denial of all the abuse that had gone on.

Gail's husband went to see her parents a little later and raised the issue of the letter. He was told that it was all rubbish, and that nothing like that had ever happened. Gail has refused to see her father since then, and will have nothing to do with him. She knows she is still frightened of him. She still experiences him as the same person who abused her and her sister. Since she wrote to them she has seen her mother only rarely, when she has been able to get away. Her mother has not denied the abuse happened, but she has not confirmed it either.

You can see that confronting the person who abused you is not always in your best interests, as it can sometimes be difficult and painful. If you want to do it, you should prepare yourself carefully. Make sure you have support from other people too, as you may be even more hurt by the response that you get from your abuser.

Whether or not to confront your abuser is a very personal choice. It's important to remember that you are doing it for yourself, hopefully to make yourself feel more powerful and to have your own history acknowledged by the people who were a part of it. If it does bring about constructive changes in the other person, then so much the better, but it's not wise to harbour unrealistic expectations of a positive outcome.

Gail and her mother have a relationship that barely works. She expected some understanding and support from her mother, and was shocked when her mother took her father's part. Where the people we have talked about in this book were abused by their fathers, whether they had confronted their fathers or not, they also had very fraught relationships with their mothers. Some, like Eva and Gail, had assumed that they had a special relationship with their mothers, and were surprised to find when they left home that their mothers no longer treated them in a special way, and were even cold and distant to them when they returned for holidays.

In some of our case histories, mothers had complained resentfully about the behaviour of their spouses, and had sworn to leave them if they continued abusing the children. Mostly they did not follow up on their affirmations and chose to stay with their partners, denying or sometimes even defending the abuse.

Gail has been able to deal with the rejection she experienced from her parents' denial of the abuse and with the shock of finding that her parents had not changed. They still do not acknowledge their own behaviour as wrong or abusive. This confirmed Gail's original experience. Her parents were never really concerned for their children's welfare, and are still not now that the children are adults.

We take the position that her father had a choice: he knew that abusing his children was wrong and went ahead and did it anyway. Their mother didn't do anything about it at the time, and carries on denying the reality of what happened even now.

Gail has been in touch with her sister Jean since the confrontation and they have formed a relationship as adults, although not a very close one. Gail still does not feel able to be completely open with her sister nor does she feel fully understood by her.

When they meet they talk a lot about their childhood, but because they have no happy memories, they have nothing very much to bond with one another about, other than the violence and abuse. Gail thinks that's why their relationship is still difficult. Jean's daughters can't understand why their aunt and mother aren't closer, as Jean is close with them. Her sister Jean lives far away, which means they cannot go to therapy together. Gail believes that if they could do that, and if they could work through some of the bad history they share, they might be able to be close at last.

She feels bad about the way that Jean was abused for so long, and guilty that she herself was 'only' abused sexually for six months. She feels that Jean took the brunt of the abuse in the family, and that her suffering spared the rest of the family from more abuse. Gail also feels bad that when she was older she did nothing to support or comfort her sister. She feels that this reflects the way the whole family behaved towards one another. None of them was able to comfort and support any of the others.

Gail is now able to form deep bonds with the other women in her women's group. She is learning to trust people and to value herself. After a lifetime of excessively high expectations of herself regarding work, she is allowing herself to spend as much time doing the things she likes to do as she spends working. She feels that she would have become mentally ill if she had not worked on herself in therapy.

This is the first time in her life that she has been able to use and enjoy time on her own and it is a very precious experience for her.

Sally is now working as a psychotherapist. Through years of therapy and group work she has gained a sense of self-esteem, although it can still be very fragile at times. She has learnt to assert herself and her needs, and to respect herself as someone important who has rights. She is learning that she no longer has to 'do it all on her own' or manage her life in an isolated way. She feels able now to ask friends for help and support.

She treats herself carefully and has learnt to protect herself when she needs to by checking out situations carefully before taking part, by getting information clearly, and by not doing things she doesn't feel good about. In many ways she has learnt to be more cautious. There are, however, still some 'blind' areas that she is aware of. She still has a strong tendency to put the needs of others, such as her family and her clients, before her own, and tries to fulfil what she imagines that other people expect of her.

From the therapy groups she takes part in she has created a network of supportive, loving friends whom she can call on when she needs to, and she increasingly does so. She feels that she has always been very much on her own up to now, and that learning to have good relationships with other people has been a major part of her growth and self-development.

After having had a nine-month period of not seeing her mother, and feeling she needed that distance in order to separate herself, she recently decided to meet her mother again. She was concerned for her mother's well-being, but she was also very clear this time that she could not 'fix' her mother's life for her. It has been very important for Sally to be able to step back and accept her mother as she is, rather than constantly hope that she will one day be able to give Sally the love and support that she was never able to give when Sally was a child.

Sally tried to talk to her mother about her grandfather abusing her. The first time she did this, her mother acted as if she didn't hear her. She persevered and told her mother again. Her mother walked away, then came back and said that she was really sorry and that she hadn't known that it had happened. She also said that she didn't want to talk about it any more. Sally found it difficult that her mother blamed herself so harshly for what had happened. She felt her mother was more preoccupied with her own guilty feelings and her own sorrow than she was with what had happened to Sally and how Sally had felt and been affected.

Whenever Sally meets any member of her family she has to remind herself not to expect anything from them in terms of affection and understanding, as she has always been disappointed. She knows now not to expect them to be on her 'wavelength', or to listen to her and empathize with her. She also knows now not to expect them to have changed in their behaviour towards her.

Sally has recently had some reconciliation with Sam, her brother, although this has been very tentative as yet. She feels that they are both 'walking towards each other' slowly and with care. Sally confronted him about his physical abuse of her some years ago and talked to him about his frequent punching and constant nastiness towards her when he came home for his school holidays. She remembers that the only time their interaction was pleasurable was when he was being sexual with her. Sally hasn't yet talked to him about his sexual abuse of her.

Sally's long-term recovery has included her being able to accept her own negative behaviour as a child, which arose from unhappiness and insecurity. She feels now that there were times when she may also have been nasty to Sam by resenting him and not wanting him in the family. When he was at boarding school, Sally had an exclusive relationship with her mother and, although it quickly changed when he came home, she believes that he must have felt very left out. She also recognizes that Sam had a very difficult time fulfilling the role of 'protector' which their grandfather had cast him into at their father's death.

Sally is now able to understand the feelings underlying the negative attitudes towards men that she has had throughout her life. In doing so, she is able to separate these feelings and attitudes from her current experiences and gradually to allow more positive experiences of the men that she meets.

She still finds it difficult to know what is appropriate behaviour with men. Having experienced so little healthy touch as a child, and having experienced so much inappropriate touch, has left Sally unable to make good judgements about what is appropriate. She is often hesitant about touching, feeling clumsy and awkward. She has overcome this feeling of awkwardness in some ways by developing skills as a massage practitioner. But when she meets men socially she still has a tendency to be very formal, as she fears she may otherwise act inappropriately somehow.

Sally recently held a party for her friends at her home. She bought a very large rocket and attached to it a rosary and cross she had been given by her grandfather. She celebrated by firing it off into the sky and watching it leave her forever.

She has finally decided that she wants to forgive her grandfather, although she feels that she can never forgive his behaviour towards her.

Dora has also decided not to see her family very much. She knew that her family would react very badly to any kind of discussion about the abuse, so instead she uses the support that she has found for herself. She sees a need to continue working on herself in groups as and when she feels ready. She is finding that as some memories come back about unhappy times in her childhood, the way is opened for still more memories to come to the surface. She finds it very comforting and healing to accept and to acknowledge these memories, talking about them to her therapist, with her friends, and in her support group.

Because Dora's parents had high academic expectations of their children, Dora has had to confront the chronic fear of failure she has always had and learn that making mistakes is a part of being human. She is learning not to condemn herself so severely. She has learnt to forgive herself and also, more recently, to treat herself as someone very precious.

The recent development of a kinder attitude within herself signified a turning-point in her recovery and in her ability to lead a happier and more comfortable life. She knows clearly nowadays that she deserves to be treated well by others, and also by herself.

Dora no longer has the fears that she once had about life, about other people and about her ability to sustain relationships. She feels better equipped to deal with life, and is more and more able to relate to others – men as well as women – in a healthy way. She has been able to begin to free herself gradually of negative beliefs about herself and the negative parental messages she still had, and which she continually used to criticise herself with. The process of freeing herself from her abusive past is continuing as she progresses through her forties feeling better about herself and more confident all the time.

For many years Dora experienced a chronic eating disorder and she had an obsession with suicide. She numbed her emotions and was very frightened of losing control over them, either in relationships or by herself. She is now learning to validate her feelings and to communicate them more clearly and assertively. She tries to remember to listen carefully to her own feelings and to accept them all as a part of her, without feeling bad about the negative parts of herself. When she does find herself reacting in situations in the ways that she used to in the past, she is learning to use this behaviour as informative and to talk it over and explore it. She is unlocking the behaviour patterns that have controlled her in her life and is gradually letting go of the parts of her that get in the way of and resist change.

Dora has taken time to test out and feel safe about all the changes she has made for herself. She now validates her 'old self' for the survival strategies she used in the past, without rejecting the part of herself that was rejected by her family. It has taken time for her to feel safe enough and whole enough to explore the negative parts of herself and the abusive way she was treated. Because of her deep feelings of worthlessness, it has taken time to see the abusive treatment as separate from herself, rather than what she deserved or somehow even a part of her.

As a child she did not have a choice. The message she got from those that treated her abusively was that she didn't count, and that her feelings were not important. She felt worthless and a part of her gave up. She describes it as a feeling of her real self ceasing to exist. She felt numbed and invisible for much of the time and deeply unhappy, living in a world that was 'fogged' and confusing and painful. She was not able to develop her own sense of personal needs and rights, or to create clear boundaries for herself.

As an adult Dora can make that choice to put her own feelings and her own needs first, and to regain a feeling of self-esteem and belonging. A part of this process is asserting her rights to fulfil her own wants and needs as a priority in her life.

She is getting clearer about what is abusive and unacceptable behaviour in her personal and professional life. She refuses to accept abuse, making a stand in whatever appropriate way she sees fit. She has been learning also to say no to unreasonable demands, which is something she has always struggled with.

She has regained enough of a sense of self-worth to be able to realize that she does not have to please everyone in order to be a worthwhile and acceptable person. She is able now to maintain a stronger sense both of herself and her boundaries.

Istra, who is now 33, is just beginning to be able to allow herself to be touched and held by close friends, and sometimes she feels able to accept a hug. Encouraged by a close friend, she has been going to a weekly massage session where the masseuse has also gently and caringly been introducing her to other healing remedies and advising her on ways of looking after herself and her body.

The positive regard she has gained from doing her very demanding job as a director of a company well has given her a huge amount of self-esteem. She has, over the years, gained a stronger sense of self-worth and has been able to look more closely at her abusive childhood.

She has recently been attending a sexuality group, having joined a similar group ten years ago. She recalls going to the first group thinking that there was nothing wrong with her and that she did not have any sexual problems. She knew that terrible things had happened to her but she didn't put herself in the category of having been sexually abused. She distanced herself from other people and was very cut off from her emotional self. She allowed herself to cry a little but never to really weep. In fact, she hated to cry, seeing it as a sign of weakness and vulnerability. She used to choke back her tears and hold her breath to stop herself crying.

Joining the original group was Istra's introduction to therapy. She knew that there was something very important in the work that they were doing there that she had to pursue, and she made an active commitment to join a follow-up group. During a further course of groupwork, she decided to change her name back to the name she had had as a child. As we said in chapter two, Istra changed her name when she was 13 as a way of disassociating herself from the small, victimized, brutalized child that she had been. Changing her name back was, for her, a way of reclaiming that small person within herself.

Istra stresses the need she has to work at her own pace

in her gradual recovery. She feels that, for her, the process of healing has been a process of reclaiming what belongs to her and she has needed the time it has taken to do this in her own way.

She has been gradually working towards the re-awakening of her feelings, and truly valuing her inner self through a rediscovery of the small child within her. She feels that it's very important for her to praise herself for each small step she has taken to reach the point she is at now. She has worked hard in groups and in her individual therapy, and then at integrating her learning into her life.

She is now reaping a harvest and her efforts are having a transforming effect on her life. She can recognize all the many small changes that have been happening. At this present time they have accumulated into solid and lasting changes, and she is beginning to experience deep feelings of joy and happiness about her life.

Istra now feels that there is a deeper meaning in all the things that have happened to her. She feels that it's not important to ascertain the 'truth' of this; if it helps her to continue working on herself and to understand and accept the life she has had so far, then it is useful.

She is at last able to give up long-term addictive habits such as heavy drinking and smoking, and also compulsive television viewing, which she used to numb herself. She has regained a feeling of being a significant part of a fascinating universe that has meaning for her.

Istra feels that she has never been very good at valuing herself or keeping for herself what is hers – either materially, in terms of belongings and money, or personally, in terms of asserting her rights and feelings. She has always been in relationships where she has given out most of the energy. Now she is getting better at negotiating space for herself and owning what is rightfully hers. She is beginning to put her own needs first instead of considering her needs to be less important than others'. She is learning to say no to what she doesn't want in her life and to state her boundaries clearly.

She has now fully accepted that she was sexually abused. In the sexuality group she is now a part of she is able to acknowledge that she is still not as in touch with herself as she would like to be, and she can clearly see how defended she used to be. This time round she is finding the group extremely hard work, and also very rewarding.

She has been able to look at the pain she suffered in childhood only very gradually and with a great deal of patience, care and understanding from the therapist she has been seeing for three years. This has enabled her to open up and to allow herself to be more vulnerable when she is with others. With her therapist she has been revisiting her childhood and feeling the pain of being very small and very brutally treated by both parents and by both her elder brothers. She has been able to cry again and recently she has been weeping a lot. Several times when working on issues around her childhood she has vomited. It has been a great release for her. She has also recently discovered that tears don't always mean sadness and has been able to cry tears of joy in her rediscovery of herself.

Throughout her life Istra has found it very difficult even to realize that she does need help, and when she does has felt unable to ask for it. She has also had great difficulty in being able to accept help that has been given to her. She sees this as a part of having not valued herself, and in small ways now she is reaching out to people that she trusts.

In her relationships with men, Istra felt that she had nothing to 'barter with'. She felt that she was not worth much and that all she had to offer was sex. She is learning to enjoy male attention now in another way and realizes that she doesn't have to be a sexual object to be appreciated.

Istra feels very let down by her parents. She copes now by distancing herself from them, and doing so has helped her to regain a strong sense of herself and her self-worth. She has finally acknowledged that she will never get from her parents the support and unconditional love that she wants and needs, and that she has to find and create this elsewhere in her life. She has also distanced herself from the younger of her two brothers, who as an adult has also acted abusively towards her. Recently she wrote him a letter, which said: 'You abused me when I was a child. You had an excuse then. We were all abused. It was an abusive environment. We're now adults and I don't put up with it any more. I had to when I was a child and I don't now. I need to spend time with people who make me feel good and you are not one of them. So I'm not going to be seeing you any more.'

Istra says, 'That's how I deal with abuse now. It happened to me once and I don't keep coming back for more as I have done in the past. It's another way that I'm getting better at looking after myself. I'm reclaiming my rights and this includes my right to respect.'

She has been sorting out amongst her friends and acquaintances those whom she wants to maintain friendships with. She is leaving behind those relationships that are abusive and those that don't nourish her. She doesn't want to stay in contact with people who don't give her as much as she can give in relationships. She is finding new and richer ways of relating, and building up lasting and caring friendships. Her abuse left her feeling that she must always put others first, that she wasn't important enough, and, for Istra, that's changing.

Istra says there was one thing that was very positive in her growing up and that was a relationship she had with a friend of her brother's. He was her first boyfriend and they lost their virginity to each other when they were both 14. He used to masturbate her until she had an orgasm, and she learnt how to masturbate herself. She focused a lot of her attention on doing this and it was a very positive experience for her. She never felt guilty about it, although she knew that her parents would disapprove. She knew that they were wrong, and she has been able to maintain a very good feeling about pleasuring herself and enjoying sex in her adult life.

Jo-Beth's experience of abuse as a young child was so traumatic that it seemed she would never recover. However, after a very painful upbringing she has fought her way back to a healthy and fulfilled life.

Jo-Beth was raped by her father at the age of four. She still has no conscious memory of that event. She knows that her mother was in hospital at the time and that her father was left to look after her and one sister, with a grandmother helping out. Some part of her said, some months after she began therapy 15 years ago, that it remembered being taken upstairs to have a bath by her father and being puzzled as to why he didn't turn on the taps.

This same part, which seemed like someone else using her mouth but not her mind, tells of his touching her, of his telling her they were going to play a game and that, if she was a good girl, he would love her. Jo-Beth had never been hugged or shown love and felt this was going to be her big chance. She would give her all for a hug. She thought a game was fun and love was a hug. What happened made her think she had got everything wrong and her mind lost its trust in itself. Her father then raped her, strangling her until she lost consciousness.

At this point Jo-Beth had an out-of-body experience where she met a being surrounded with light. She spoke to this being in her mind, pleading to be allowed to stay, but was told wordlessly that she had to go back.

Her father put her into a very hot bath and she passed out again. During the night she had a feeling there was something big still inside her and she wet the bed. The part of her that has the memory says that her father had threatened to kill her if she told and, when her grandmother came into her bedroom the following morning and was angry about the wet bed, she tried to tell indirectly by saying, 'Daddy made me do it.' Her grandmother told her not to be so stupid. She explains that, at that point, an impenetrable steel shutter came down in her mind. As that already fractured child, she lost her sense of self, of having a mind or a body.

Jo-Beth thinks there was probably oral abuse later on but she hasn't yet any clear memory of that. When her father died some years ago, she was the only one who was sad because she had hoped that one day he would talk to her and help her remember what he had done. At his funeral, as she watched the coffin disappear, she recited over and over to herself, 'You can't hurt me any more', desperately wanting to believe it.

As a teenager and during the 10 years she was suicidal as an adult, her longing to hang herself, which she knew would start as something awful but would lead her to find love, was one part of the long-term damage that resulted from the abuse. On some deep level, she had come to believe that a hug was having something tight round her throat until she died.

She did not have any actual memory of the abuse until her mid-forties, when she started therapy. Even then, the memories that came were ones she found difficult to believe, although she heard herself telling them. She had a series of therapists. In her late fifties she met a therapist who, after some time, was able to recognize that she was a multiple personality. This recognition changed Jo-Beth's life. It made sense of so much of her experience, of her inner chaos, of her not having any memories, and gave her a stability within herself that she had never had before. Thanks to help she has received from this therapist and a multiple-personality friend, she can now think and believe her own thoughts without a 'barrage' of inner voices destroying her thinking.

Jo-Beth's father's abuse of her caused a physical injury which led to a temporary limp. This injury later turned into a TB hip joint and, from her early teens, she spent four years in hospitals. This was disastrous because school and study had been important and stabilizing for her; her achievements had begun to give her a sense of self. She had no schooling during those four years and her dreams of eventually going to university were shattered. Her years in hospital were very damaging and she has many memories of being cruelly and abusively treated.

She had two breakdowns during that time in hospital. In the first one, there was someone in the ward dying of cancer of the throat, and Jo-Beth felt in a state of terror and as though she was being strangled all the time. It was not until therapy more than 30 years later that she realized this had been the partial surfacing of a deeply hidden memory. Part of the treatment for this, in addition to drugs, was that she was laughed at for her fears. It taught her that it was safer to keep her fears to herself, so she told no one the next time something similar happened. She had two further breakdowns, in her twenties and early forties. These were much more severe and long lasting.

Jo-Beth's has been a difficult and lonely journey, a loneliness aggravated by her increasing disability, and she has had to do much of it for herself. When she first heard herself saying she had been abused, she thought she was crazy, because she had never heard of it happening. It was some years after she began therapy that she saw a film called *Ruth* about sexual abuse and realized that she was not mad after all. Before then, it was not out in the open, not talked about.

She has been having therapy with various therapists for 15 years now, something she began soon after the beginning of her last breakdown because she wanted to find out why she was ill. She struggled and fought to get the help she knew she needed. For some years she saw a therapist who made her ill and was abusive to her.

With the therapist she has been seeing for three years now, she has felt heard and understood in a way she had not experienced before, and is very aware of the importance of having her abuse acknowledged and her own personal experience believed and validated. Jo-Beth feels that this therapist has been the first safe attachment in her life. With him, she is now exploring the range of her personalities and working at healing the extreme dissociation this event caused. She feels that her struggle to heal herself was not really a matter of choice but an absolute necessity, and that it has been both a terrible and a worthwhile journey.

She works in London as a psychotherapist and has a library of information about abuse and its effects, and about

153

multiple personalities. She is married with a family and lives an increasingly fulfilling and stable life in a house equipped to help her cope with her disabilities.

She feels in awe of the indestructibility of the self, the core reality within each of us that can never be destroyed. She is conscious of an inner wisdom within herself which has somehow enabled her to survive, to search for and know the help she needed, and to help her in her healing journey.

Jo-Beth talks about the 'ISH' level of selves that are in multiple personalities, the wise 'Inner Self Helpers' who know and help the person to survive. She feels that there must be something like that in everyone, and that one aspect of good therapy is to help a person get in touch with that inner knowing. She has had to learn to trust herself and recognize what is right for herself, and says, 'If I want to help someone, I have to accept them as and where they are.' She feels there must be many who are like she was, suffering with depression and breakdowns and with no conscious memory of being abused, and she believes that there *is* a way out of the place abused people have been driven to within themselves.

Roger had been in therapy for several years, and the work he had done on himself had already paid many dividends, when he recovered his memories of sexual abuse. First he remembered the incident with the man at the derelict house, and then other memories of abuse came back. This is common for survivors: the original abuse is so well buried that it takes a while for it to surface, and then other memories follow it. Roger likens the process to 'one of those magic tricks: the magician pulls on a string and a flag appears, and then one flag follows another until the stage has a whole pile of flags on it.' Not everybody has a 'pile of flags', but it's an analogy that makes sense to Roger as he continues to remember incidents of sexual abuse.

Roger still has to be careful not to let himself be abused. He accepts that being careful is what it takes to be free and to keep feeling good about himself.

One of the major issues for him in therapy has been to recognize the very mixed messages he got from his adoptive parents, and how that has affected his self-esteem. He took on their view of the world. They saw the world as a dangerous place where they as a family were the small people who could not expect very much. They taught him not to make a fuss, and that he was usually in the wrong. On top of this came his experience of being sexually abused, sometimes by people he trusted and sometimes by complete strangers. He did not feel that he had the right to make a safe boundary for himself.

His adoptive mother encouraged him to think of himself as special, to think of himself as 'a good boy', and told him that no matter what he did, he was fundamentally good. He now sees that these messages from his adoptive mother were often just a manipulation to try to get him to be 'a good boy' and that she was basically being dishonest with him. He did feel very good with her at the time, and still feels loved and nurtured by her when he thinks back to their relationship. So this 'loved' and 'good' boy also got the message that he had to accept being abused as part of his life, and that he had no real right to stand up for himself or for what he wanted.

These mixed messages led to his being secretive. Whenever he did go to his adoptive parents for help, they were either dismissive and disbelieving, or so shocked that they seemed to be more concerned with the trouble he brought than to help him sort out a situation. The end result was that from eight or nine years old he kept his problems to himself and he learned to lie.

In his therapy the issue of his keeping secrets and not talking about what is going on for him has been a continual problem, both for him and for the people who share his life. He has been self-reliant to the point of isolation.

People whom he withholds from still get angry with him, and he used to see that as confirmation that the best thing to do is keep quiet. He now recognizes this is wrong, and he has learned to be more open with people generally. He has reached a point where he feels supported by the people he shares his thoughts and feelings with, rather than feeling a need to defend himself by keeping secrets.

He has learned to trust more generally, and sees the world as a far safer place than he once experienced it as being. This in turn leaves him able to feel that he can enjoy his own life and be easier around the other people in it. He can now accept and trust family and friends and be part of a family situation in a way that he was unable to before. He is less critical and blaming, and less suspicious that people in his life are out to take things from him.

He is able to share more in every sense than he did before. As he feels more secure in himself, so he is able to be more generous and less mean. He can allow people to come and stay in his home in a way that he was never able to before. He is hospitable rather than insecure and distrustful, and is interested in being sociable rather than unsociable. He still feels sensitive about his time and space, and is careful not to oversocialize and feel invaded.

As he has 'grown up' (his words), he has become able to relate to children as children, rather than competing with them for attention as if they were his rivals, which is how he used experience them. He enjoys giving to children and others, without losing his sense of himself and his own wants and needs. He believes that this is a vital balance to keep, so he doesn't feel resentful of the time and space he gives to friends and family. He also recognizes that he needs less time being 'separate' than he did before.

He has learned to be more sensitive and less dismissive of the experience of others as he has worked on himself. He is generally less critical than he once was, and that is another way he has found of feeling generous inside rather than uptight. He believes that many men who have been sexually abused as children have similar issues, which they stay defended about, even denying the hurt to themselves. He believes that working through the feelings he had as a result of being sexually abused has helped him to overcome his isolation and defensiveness, and to get clearer about the general effects of being brought up with real confusion about himself.

Each of the people we have talked about has struggled through their lives to survive the effects of their abuse and their abusive upbringings, and for each the struggle was enormous and painful.

From sexual innuendo to flashing, from fondling to rape, all sexual abuse has deep and lasting effects on children. It distorts their whole life experience.

As adults, we need to learn to value and to listen to our own inner child. We must look at ourselves and our past experiences in a caring way, allowing the small person that is within us to unlock the doors of repression and express some of the emotions we have had within us from childhood.

We also need to fully understand the effects on children

of belittling them and of denying them their true experience and feelings. We need to be able to be there for them with an understanding of how significant their childhood experiences are, and of how hurtful and confusing it is for a child when they are not heard or listened to.

We need to have consistency in the way we treat children, giving them firm, clear boundaries and always enabling clear channels of communication, allowing them to express the range of their emotions, including anger and rage, and letting them know that they are safe and loved by us.

There is no such thing as 'minimal' abuse. 'It only happened once, or twice, or three times' is once or twice or three times too many. Any single abuse has an appalling effect on a young life. If we work out our own issues that have come from being abused, and speak out against abuse, we can make people aware of how much of it goes on, and we can watch out for and protect our children.

We wrote this book hoping to make a difference, and we hope this book makes a difference to you in your life. If we, and you, together can help to stop any child from being abused in any way, we will have made an enormous difference to that child's whole life.

Further Reading

Bradshaw, John, *The Family*, Deerfield Beach, Florida, Health
  Communications, 1987.
  Healing the Shame that Binds You, Deerfield Beach, Florida,
  Health Communications, 1988.
Engel, Beverley, *The Right to Innocence*, Los Angeles, California,
  Jeremy P. Tarcher, 1989.
Masson, Jeffrey, *Freud: The Assault on Truth*, New York, Farrar,
  Straus & Giroux, 1984; London, Faber and Faber, 1984.
Miller, Alice, *The Drama of Being a Child*, London, Virago, 1987.
  Banished Knowledge, London, Virago, 1991.
Sanford, Linda T., *Strong at the Broken Places*, New York, Random
  House, 1990; London, Virago, 1991.
Satir, Virginia, *The New Peoplemaking*, Mountain View, California,
  Science and Behavior Books, 1988.